HUME'S NAT~~URALISM~~

Books on Hume's philosophy invariably fall into one or the other of two categories. Either they are intended for specialists, with references to secondary literature and endless footnotes, or they are formulaic textbooks, following Hume point by point. Neither of these types of book cater for the beginner. H. O. Mounce's book is unusual in that it offers the broad picture of Hume's work without loading it down with scholarly detail.

Admirably clear and coherent, *Hume's Naturalism* is the ideal starting point for any student coming to Hume's work for the first time. Analysing Hume's most famous works, *A Treatise of Human Nature* and *Dialogues Concerning Natural Religion* in close detail, this book will make it possible for general readers to grasp the broader picture of Hume's work so that when they return to the textual details, they have a better sense of their significance.

H. O. Mounce is Senior Lecturer in Philosophy at the University of Wales, Swansea. He is well known for his brilliant introduction to Wittgenstein's *Tractatus*. His other publications include *The Two Pragmatisms: From Peirce to Rorty* and *Moral Practices* (with D. Z. Phillips), both published by Routledge.

HUME'S NATURALISM

H. O. Mounce

London and New York

First published 1999
by Routledge
11 New Fetter Lane, London EC4P 4EE

Simultaneously published in the USA and Canada
by Routledge
29 West 35th Street, New York, NY 10001

Typeset in Bembo by Routledge
Printed and bound in Great Britain by
Mackays of Chatham PLC, Chatham, Kent

British Library Cataloguing in Publication Data
A catalogue record for this book is available from the British Library

Library of Congress Cataloging in Publication Data
A catalogue record for this book has been requested

ISBN 0–415–19124–6 (hbk)
ISBN 0–415–19125–4 (pbk)

FOR CAROLA

CONTENTS

PREFACE

This study is intended primarily for the general reader, not for the specialist. To such a reader the philosophy of Hume presents special difficulties. They belong to the whole rather than to any specific part. Paragraph by paragraph, Hume's work presents few difficulties, for he is amongst the most lucid writers in philosophy. The difficulties lie in grasping the basic drift, the general philosophy that underlines the work. These difficulties are not removed by the standard textbook, which follows Hume point by point, for the effect of such a work is precisely to submerge the reader in detail, to lose the wood in the trees. One may find, it is true, many specialist works which convey an interpretation of the whole philosophy. But these are addressed to other specialists and abound in discussions of secondary sources which the ordinary reader cannot follow. What is needed is a work which aims, not to pit one interpretation against others, but simply to convey a view of the whole that is coherent and, above all, clear. That is what is attempted in the present study. I have taken a theme which is central to Hume's work (that of the relation between naturalism and empiricism) and I have used it to illumi-nate the whole. My interpretation is based on a study of Hume that covers almost forty years and I am confident that I can defend it against others. But it is not the purpose of this study to do so. What is important is that my inter-pretation should enable readers to get their bearings. Later they may adopt another, which they think better. Still, it will have served its purpose. For, having given readers a view of the whole, it will have given them the basis for evaluating any interpretation.

A certain minimum of scholarly discussion and criticism is unavoidable. But I have confined this mainly to the first chapter, where I have explained the sources of my interpretation, how it arose in the history of Hume scholar-ship and how it has sometimes been misunderstood. The body of the book consists in the application of this interpretation to Hume's chief masterpieces, *A Treatise of Human Nature* and *Dialogues Concerning Natural Religion*. As I have explained, it is not my purpose in the present study to engage with the numerous commentators on Hume. Nevertheless, I have attempted to keep the reader informed about other studies, both where they support and where they conflict with my own.

For the second time in recent years Ian Tipton has given me the benefit of his scholarship in reading my work in manuscript and Helen Baldwin, with her usual efficiency, has prepared it for publication. My thanks are due to them both.

1

INTRODUCTION
The scholarly background

The importance of naturalism in understanding Hume's philosophy was first emphasized by Kemp Smith. Kemp Smith's work has been available for more than fifty years[1] but it has not had the influence one might have anticipated. Amongst specialists on Hume, it has certainly had an influence. But amongst philosophers in general, at least until very recently, it has been largely ignored. It is still very common, for example, to find references to 'Humean Causation'. This is the view that causation is identical with regularity or constant conjunction. The implication is that Hume held this view. It is not uncommon to find people who assume that Hume denied the existence of causation altogether. Kemp Smith spent some time in demolishing both those views. My own interpretation of Hume differs from Kemp Smith's but it is greatly indebted to him and it will be useful therefore to consider, first, what interpretation he advanced, and second, why it has not been widely influential.

The interpretation of Hume most commonly accepted in the nineteenth century was advanced by Thomas Reid and, later, by T. H. Green.[2] In his *Inquiry*, Reid argued with great power and clarity that the empiricism of the eighteenth century rested on what he termed the theory of ideas. Roughly speaking, this is the view that our knowledge of objects is derived from the ideas or images which they impress on our minds. It is these ideas or images which are the immediate objects of perception, not the objects in an independent world which they represent. Reid argued that this view led inevitably to scepticism, for unless we already have knowledge of an independent world how can we know that it is represented by our images or ideas? He argued, further, that the whole view rested on a fallacy. The ideas or images, to which the empiricists refer, are really the sensory experience involved in perceiving an object. This sensory experience is that *whereby* we perceive; it is not *what* we perceive. The empiricists confuse the two. Thus the sensory experience involved in perceiving a tree, that *whereby* it is perceived, is identified with the object of perception, *what* is perceived. In effect, the object of perception becomes our own sensory experience, which comes between ourselves and the tree.

The scepticism implicit in this view is not apparent in every empiricist. But that is because not every empiricist is consistent. It is here that we may appreciate the virtue of Hume. Unlike earlier empiricists, he follows the implications of the empiricist view and makes explicit the scepticism it contains. In his philosophy, we are deprived of our certainty not simply in an independent world but even in the reality of the self. The only reality are the ideas or impressions themselves.

For Reid, then, the virtue of Hume lies in his making explicit the scepticism inherent in empiricism, thereby, though unwittingly, reducing it to absurdity. But Reid was concerned not simply to expose the fallacies of empiricism; he wished also to replace it with a quite different philosophy. This was the naturalism which is found already in Shaftesbury but which was developed most clearly by philosophers in the Scottish school, such as Hutcheson, Turnbull, Kames, Reid himself and, later, William Hamilton. The essence of Scottish naturalism is that our knowledge has its source not in our experience or reasoning but in our relations to a world which transcends both our knowledge and ourselves. The power of this view may be illustrated by referring once more to empiricism. The empiricist view is that our knowledge has its source in sense experience. Thus our belief counts as knowledge only if we can justify it. We justify a belief by stepping outside it and comparing it with what we observe in the world. This view overlooks a point of some importance. The power of comparing a belief with the world itself presupposes beliefs about the world. We cannot step outside all our beliefs. This means that we cannot justify our knowledge as a whole, though we may justify one belief by reference to others. 'Belief' said William Hamilton 'is the primary condition of reason, not reason the ultimate ground of belief'.[3] The Scottish naturalists clearly anticipated views which were later developed by Kant. Thus our ideas or beliefs cannot simply be the product of sense experience since without ideas or beliefs our sense experience is blind. The point may be illustrated by reference to our belief in an independent world. On the empiricist view, this belief is justified by an inference from sense experience. But sense experience, being subjective, can give us no idea of an independent world. If we have no idea of such a world, how can we infer it? The inference from sense experience is plausible only if we already have knowledge of such a world. But if we already have such knowledge, it is unnecessary to make the inference. We could never have known an independent world were it not *given* to us in *natural* belief. For it is the *condition* of all our knowledge. It is naturalism in this sense which Reid opposes to the empiricism, as he sees it, of Hume's philosophy.

Now one of the main objects of Kemp Smith's study is to show that Reid's interpretation of Hume is mistaken. He argues that Hume was already aware of the scepticism inherent in empiricism and that the aim of his philosophy was not to advance but rather to counteract that scepticism, on the basis of views which in many respects were similar to Reid's own. As evidence for this, Kemp Smith argues that the *Treatise* is misleading in its arrangement, so that to appreciate the flow of its argument one needs, as it were, to read it backwards. In the first book, we are presented with views in epistemology which are empiricist in their tendency; in the last, with views on morals which are plainly influenced by the naturalism of Hutcheson. Kemp Smith argues that the views in the first book are merely provisional; it is the views in the last which are fundamental to the *Treatise* as a whole. Thus Hutcheson had argued that morality arises not through reasoning but on the basis of feelings given to us by nature. In morals, reason is the slave of the passions. The originality of the *Treatise* is that Hume takes this view and applies it quite generally, so that reason is everywhere subordinate to feeling, not simply in morals but even in matters of fact. In all our knowledge, we depend ultimately on natural attitude or belief. What the *Treatise* presents, in short, is not empiricism but a thoroughgoing naturalism. To appreciate the force of Hume's view we may compare it with a view of man which had become common during the enlightenment. The leading thinkers of the enlightenment accepted the Greek definition of man as a rational animal; in other words, they assumed that man is moved primarily by reason, the feelings being subordinate, serving to help or hinder reason in its operation. Hume exactly reverses this view.[4] Reason is always subordinate in its operation to feeling or beliefs, which have their origin in our nature and are not themselves derived from reason. The implication of this view is the opposite of sceptical. The essence of scepticism is that it seeks through reason to undermine our fundamental beliefs. Hume's point is that reason is cogent only when it is subordinate to our fundamental beliefs. Consequently it cannot undermine them. Thus in discussing our belief in an independent world his aim is not to undermine that belief. His point is precisely that reason cannot undermine a belief which is implanted in us by nature. The belief in an independent world, being prior to reason, is impervious to it.

> Thus the sceptic still continues to reason and believe even tho' he asserts, that he cannot defend his reason by reason….Nature has not left this to his choice, and has doubtless esteemed it an affair of too great importance to be trusted to our uncertain reasonings and speculations. We may well ask, *What causes induce us to believe in the existence of body?* but 'tis in vain to ask *Whether there be body or not?* That is a point, which we must take for granted in all our reasonings.[5]

At the heart of Hume's philosophy in the *Treatise* is his analysis of causality. Kemp Smith supports his interpretation of Hume by a brilliant account of this analysis. It must be taken in two stages. In the first, Hume takes an instance of the causal process, for example, one ball's moving another, and seeks to detect the features essential to it. He immediately detects two such features, contiguity and succession. The first ball is in contact with the second (contiguity); the movement of the second follows upon contact with the first (succession). But these features, though necessary to our idea of causality, are not sufficient. A mere succession does not in itself strike us as causal. Hume detects a third feature, constant conjunction. When the process is repeated, the same thing occurs. It is clear, however, that constant conjunction can reveal no feature that is not already known. For it is a mere repetition of the process already detected. That concludes the first stage of the analysis. It is essential to note, first, that Hume has confined himself throughout to what can be detected in the causal process simply by observation or sense experience and, second, that the conclusion is entirely negative. Our knowledge of causality cannot be derived simply from sense experience. In short, the conclusion is the opposite of empiricist. Observation of the external world cannot in itself reveal what is essential to causality. In particular, it cannot reveal what is most essential, namely, its *necessity*. What convinces us that a process is causal is not a mere succession in the events; rather it is the feeling that when the first event occurs the second is *bound* to follow. We feel the events *always* occur that way. The question is how we can detect what will always occur, simply by observing what occurs here and now. The answer is that we cannot.

Hume now moves to the second stage of his analysis. Having considered and found unsatisfactory what we observe in the external process, he next considers what occurs in our minds when we observe that process. What appears in sense experience is insufficient; we must now consider what we may contribute to what appears. Here we have the essentials, it may be noted, of Kant's Copernican revolution.[6] To elucidate our knowledge, it is insufficient to consider what appears in the world; we must consider how the mind takes what appears to it. Thus, on Hume's analysis, there is a tendency, instinctive or natural to the mind, to trust repeated occurrence. Having experienced one event repeatedly follow another, we *feel* on observing the first that the second is bound to follow. Our idea of causality is based on this feeling, which is habitual or instinctive to the mind. What appears in sense experience as constant conjunction is turned by the mind into the form of causality. But the workings of the mind are instinctive or natural. They are not based on any rational insight into the objective nature of the causal process. On a matter of this importance, nature has not trusted to our fallible reasonings and speculations. Thus our reasoning about matters of fact can proceed only when the mind already takes the world in the form of causality, only when it is already adjusted to the causal process. The adjustment itself is prior to reason. It follows that our understanding of the world is based on relations which arise from the workings of nature, not from those of our own understanding.

This takes us to the heart of Hume's philosophy. The aim of the *Treatise* is to draw the limits of human reason, thereby providing the cure both for scepticism and for speculative metaphysics. The speculative metaphysician, assuming an unlimited power in human reason, seeks through its exercise to discover the ultimate nature of the universe. But he soon encounters problems, baffling in their nature, which he solves by an exercise rather of his imagination than of his reason. Consequently, what we find in speculative metaphysics is a proliferation of systems, each having as much or as little authority as any of the others. Philosophical scepticism arises as a recoil from this situation. Finding himself perplexed by insoluble problems, the philosopher takes refuge in universal doubt. The cure for both these tendencies is a proper understanding of the nature, and therefore of the limits, of human reason. Reason is cogent only when it derives its power from our natural beliefs, the ultimate causes of which are entirely unknown. Scepticism is dissipated when it is understood that reason, being relative to those beliefs, cannot undermine them. Speculative metaphysics is dissipated when it is understood that reason is inevitably limited by the beliefs to which it is relative. In this respect, the analysis of causality is exemplary. In causality we have a process which enters at every moment into all our affairs. But we have no insight into the nature of the process. It carries us in all our reasonings, but we do not know what carries us. For nature has equipped us to respond to causality, not to understand it. The moral is obvious.

> While we cannot give a satisfactory reason why we believe, after a thousand experiments, that a stone will fall or fire burn, can we ever satisfy ourselves concerning any determination which we may form with regard to the origin of worlds and the situation of nature from and to eternity?[7]

The conclusion of a sound philosophy, therefore, is that we should confine our reasonings to where they may be fruitful, to those aspects of human and physical nature which we are given to understand.

Imperfections

Through a redistribution of emphases, Kemp Smith has turned Hume from an empiricist into a Scottish naturalist. His study belongs amongst those great works of scholarship, through which our understanding of a subject is not simply increased but rather transformed. Why then has his work not been more widely influential? There are various factors. Some of them belong to the circumstances of the time. His work appeared in 1941, when the philosophical world was preoccupied with logical positivism.[8] Kemp Smith belonged to an older generation and was associated with idealism, a philosophy commonly thought to be discredited. The logical positivists had an allegiance to empiricism, of which their philosophy was a development, and they took Hume as one of their champions. The minority who opposed empiricism took Hume at this estimate and were more concerned to criticize than to understand him. Moreover, Kemp Smith's contrast between empiricism and naturalism did not appear to the philosopher of the time as a contrast. The naturalism of the Scottish school was not understood. The only naturalism available was the scientific naturalism of the logical positivists, which was a development of empiricism. At the time, there was no apparent contrast.

But these are factors which belong to the circumstances of the time. The more important factors, for our purpose, are those which arise from certain imperfections in Kemp Smith's own work. There are two such imperfections, and each must be considered in some detail. The first concerns the consistency of Hume's naturalism. As we have seen, Kemp Smith recognizes that the opening sections of the *Treatise* are empiricist in their tendency. He argues, however, that these views are merely provisional and that they are properly understood only when they are supplemented by the views which occur later. The trouble is that empiricism and naturalism, of the Scottish type, are not simply different but incompatible, so that it is difficult to see how one can arrive at the latter simply by supplementing the former. For the Scottish naturalist, the mind is to be understood in its relations to a world which transcends it. For the eighteenth-century empiricist, the world is to be understood through its reflections in the mind. For the naturalist, the relations between mind and world are intentional or teleological. For the empiricist, the world impresses itself on the mind in a manner which is quasi-mechanical. For the naturalist, the mind reveals its capacities precisely in our dealings with an independent world. For the empiricist, the mind is characterized by what is private or subjective. The naturalist has no problem about the existence of the independent world, since the existence of such a world provides the setting for his whole philosophy. The empiricist, having characterized the mind, has great difficulty in showing how it can know an independent world.

It is impossible to combine those views in a coherent philosophy. If there is a philosophy which contains both, we must reject some of its aspects in favour of others. Now Kemp Smith's tendency is to take Hume's philosophy as a whole. Either he is an empiricist, as Reid supposes, or he is a naturalist, as Kemp Smith supposes himself. But one of the most striking features of the *Treatise*, the source perhaps of its enduring appeal, is that it vividly expresses the processes of philosophical perplexity, the condition in which the mind is torn between incompatible views. This is most vividly expressed in the section where Hume himself falls into the scepticism from which at the beginning of the section he had promised to deliver us.

> I begun this subject with premising, that we ought to have an implicit faith in our senses, and that this wou'd be the conclusion, I shou'd draw from the whole of my reasoning. But to be ingenuous, I feel myself *at present* of a quite contrary sentiment, and am more inclin'd to repose no faith at all in my senses, or rather imagination, than to place in it such an implicit confidence.[9]

Overall clarity or coherence is not the most evident feature of Hume's philosophy.[10] In this, he is greatly inferior to Thomas Reid. Reid's philosophy is based on a systematic criticism of the philosophical assumptions common to his age and, in particular, of the empiricist scheme which Hume adopts at the beginning of the *Treatise*. Hume himself seems never to have considered such a criticism. The scheme was commonly accepted by the philosophers of the age and he took it as established. It allows him some room for manoeuvre. In particular, he makes good use of the distinction between impressions of reflection and impressions of sensation. Impressions of reflection, from which we get our ideas of the passions, are not really reflections of sensory impressions but have an independent power. They are more properly impressions of reaction. In this way, Hume is able to give the mind a more active cast than one might at first suppose. Moreover, since our most fundamental ideas arise from ideas of reflection, rather than from those of sensation, he is enabled in some measure to break free from the empiricist scheme. But the scheme is still quite inadequate to his purposes. The naturalism to which Kemp Smith refers is really present in Hume's philosophy and constitutes its most profound aspects. But empiricism is also present and is incompatible with the naturalism. In consequence the *Treatise* continually presents us with an acute tension between incompatible philosophies.

The point will be illustrated in more detail as we proceed but even at this stage it will be useful to give two illustrations. First, the naturalist view evidently requires an intentional view of belief. Belief takes an object and presupposes a world independent of itself. Hume, following the empiricist scheme, defines belief in purely subjective terms. Thus belief differs from the imagination simply through the greater vivacity of its ideas. Kemp Smith argues that Hume's aim is not to identify belief with vivacity. His aim is simply to indicate one way in which belief may be distinguished from the imagination. However, Hume never says this, which is somewhat remarkable. What is even more remarkable is that he says the exact opposite. 'Thus it appears, that *belief* or *assent*, which always attends the memory and senses, is nothing but the vivacity of those perceptions they present; and that this alone distinguishes them from the imagination.'[11]

Second, Hume treats an idea on the model of an image, which copies an impression. Now the impression which gives rise to the idea of causality belongs to the internal sense, being an impression of reflection. Since an idea is the mere copy of an impression then, strictly speaking, our ideas of causality should represent the workings of our own minds. Moreover there is a passage in which this is what Hume says: 'Upon the whole, necessity is something that exists in the mind, not in objects; nor is it possible for us ever to form the most distant idea of it, considered as a quality in bodies.'[12] Kemp Smith is correct to argue that this passage misrepresents the main drift of Hume's analysis and he holds on this basis that it should be discounted. But in a coherent naturalism the passage would not have appeared at all.

Once the inconsistencies in Hume's philosophy are appreciated, it becomes easy to remove a problem which Kemp Smith himself never addressed. As he recognizes, the philosophy he attributes to Hume is very similar to that of Thomas Reid. On any serious estimate, Reid was a philosopher of great ability and he spent a number of years in studying the *Treatise*. It is remarkable he never notices that its views were very similar to his own. The problem disappears once one recognizes that the *Treatise* involves assumptions which are quite incompatible with Reid's views. As we have seen, those assumptions appear at the beginning of the work. It is natural to read an author in the light of his opening assumptions. Read in this way, the views which appear later in the work seem reconcilable with the earlier ones only by taking them as ironic in expression and sceptical in intent. Moreover, it is very easy to take them in that way. We may illustrate the point by referring to what Hume says about the relation between reason and our natural beliefs. On a close study, these remarks reveal themselves as essentially epistemological. Reason depends in part for its very cogency or power on those beliefs. That is a remark about the nature of reason. But read in the light of the earlier views, the remarks seem merely psychological. As it happens, we cannot help holding those beliefs; nevertheless we have no good reason to do so. Here reason and natural beliefs are in conflict. For Reid the two are in harmony, reason, so far as it is cogent, having its very base in natural belief. We may grant that this also is Hume's view in the *Treatise*. But it is not surprising that even Reid failed to find it there, and that itself testifies to a lack of coherence in Hume's naturalism.

The second imperfection in Kemp Smith's work is that he fails to distinguish between two quite different types of naturalism. The naturalism which appears in the profounder aspects of Hume's work is quite different from the scientific naturalism or positivism which developed much later, during the course of the nineteenth century. But Kemp Smith never distinguishes clearly between the two and sometimes treats them as interchangeable. In this way, he obliterates or renders obscure his contrast between empiricism and naturalism, for scientific naturalism is a development of empiricism. This is a point of vital importance and we must consider it in some detail.

The naturalism which appears in the profounder aspects of Hume's work is the same as that of the Scottish naturalists. This is essentially *epistemological*. It holds that the source of our knowledge lies not in our own experience or reasoning but in our relations to the world, which for the most part pass beyond our knowledge. These relations show themselves in capacities, attitudes and beliefs which are not derived from experience and reasoning. Reasoning is cogent and experience intelligible only so far as they presuppose those capacities, attitudes and beliefs. Thus in all our experience or reasoning we presuppose our belief in causality or in an independent world. These are natural beliefs. They are formed in us along with ourselves and therefore have their source not in our own activity but in the world which has produced us.

Scientific naturalism, or positivism, is a doctrine about the nature of reality as a whole. It is essentially *metaphysical*, though it often takes the guise of an attack on metaphysics. It holds that reality is co-extensive with nature. Nature itself is defined as that which falls under the categories of physical science. Since nature falls within those categories and since it is co-extensive with reality, the whole of reality, in principle at least, may be revealed by scientific inquiry. Science therefore embraces all knowledge. It proceeds by framing laws which are derived from sense experience. The source of our knowledge, therefore, lies wholly within our own experience and reasoning. The doctrine in an extreme form appears in the following definition by John Dewey. According to Dewey, naturalism is the view 'that the whole of the universe or experience may be accounted for by a method like that of the physical sciences'.[13] We may note that for Dewey experience is interchangeable with the whole universe and that the physical sciences provide a method by which it may be wholly revealed.

It should be evident that the above doctrine is not simply different from Scottish naturalism but entirely incompatible with it. Scientific naturalism is an expression of the Sophistic view that man is the measure of all things; Scottish naturalism is a denial of that view, the measure being in nature, not in man. The first naturalism has an unbounded confidence in human reason and experience; the second an awareness of their inevitable limits. The first supposes that belief is measured by reason; the second that reason rests ultimately on belief. The first supposes that the whole universe may be known on the basis of familiar categories; the second that our categories rest on causes which transcend both our categories and ourselves. For the first, the universe is merely an extension of what is already known; for the second, it is ultimately mysterious. The first is secular in spirit; the second, is religious.

The *Treatise*, in its profounder aspects, can be taken as a criticism of scientific naturalism. Thus in his introduction, Hume makes clear that his aim is to cure the disorders of philosophy. The source of these disorders lies precisely in the view that nothing is mysterious but only problematical and that any difficulty may be removed, given sufficient persistence, by human reason. It is this which gives rise to speculative metaphysics and, by a recoil, to philosophical scepticism. Against this, Hume argues that reason is inevitably limited and that a recognition of what we cannot understand is the requirement of a sound philosophy. Only in this way can we provide the cure for philosophical scepticism on the one hand and speculative metaphysics on the other.

The scientific naturalists, it is true, were also hostile to metaphysics. But that is because they thought it unnecessary, having been replaced by science. The metaphysicians had adopted inappropriate methods in their attempt to discover the ultimate nature of the universe. With the development of science, a method has at last been found which is adequate to the purpose. Their view, in short, is that science does the same job as metaphysics but with different and more appropriate methods. Thus Dewey, as we have seen, takes for granted that the physical sciences provide a method by which we may explain the whole of reality. In effect, this is to adopt a *metaphysical interpretation of science*.

We may illustrate the point by contrasting the attitude of the two naturalisms to Newtonian mechanics. In the nineteenth century, the Newtonian system was commonly treated, not as a model for understanding certain features of the physical world, but as a definitive picture of the whole universe. It is this view which played a large part in the rise of scientific naturalism. The attitude of Hume and the Scottish naturalists was radically different. They valued Newton because, in contrast, for example, to the Cartesians, he removed from science not simply metaphysical methods but also the metaphysical task. In their terms, he refused to speculate about *ultimate* causes and confined himself to what is *manifest*. This distinction between the manifest and the ultimate, which is reminiscent of Kant's distinction between the phenomenal and the noumenal, is fundamental to their attitude. The distinction appears, in various forms, at innumerable points in the *Treatise*. For example, within a single section, the one on causality, it appears more than a dozen times. The *ultimate* arouses our *curiosity*, which, like any other passion, is remorseless once aroused. Frustrated in one theory, it readily manufactures another and will accept any theory rather than remain unsatisfied. In this way, there arises that proliferation of theories which corrupt science and philosophy alike. The cure is to confine our inquiries to what we are fitted to understand, to what can be made *manifest* to our faculties. This is what Hume and the Scottish naturalists took to be Newton's method. He refused to manufacture hypotheses, to speculate about ultimate causes, and confined his experiments to those aspects of nature which may be made manifest. In his *History of England*, Hume praises Newton for some of his positive achievements. But Newton's supreme achievement he takes to be *negative*. He curbed the vanity of the learned by showing that nature, so far from conforming to their speculations, is ultimately transcendent.

> Boyle was a great partisan of the mechanical philosophy; a theory which, by discovering some of the secrets of nature, and allowing us to imagine the rest, is agreeable to the natural vanity and curiosity of men....While Newton seemed to draw off the veil from some of the mysteries of nature, he showed at the same time the imperfections of the mechanical philosophy; and thereby restored her ultimate secrets to that obscurity in which they ever did and ever will remain.[14]

In the light of the above passage, it is worth noting that some commentators have taken Hume himself to be a partisan of the mechanical philosophy. Some, indeed, have argued that he hoped by means of the principles of association to institute a thoroughgoing science of human nature, in the manner of the scientific naturalists.[15] In fact, Hume was always clear that the mechanisms of association were a surface phenomenon. In other words, they belonged to those aspects of mind which can be made manifest. He never supposed that they would enable us to explain the mind in its ultimate causes. Moreover, by the time he wrote the *Enquiries*, he had become convinced that even his earlier estimate of their importance was exaggerated.

Given that scientific and Scottish naturalism stand in such stark contrast, one may wonder how the one could ever have been confused with the other. The answer lies in the increasing domination of scientific naturalism. It is now acquired with the culture and for most intellectuals is the only available faith. Thus although the modern commentator repeatedly misrepresents the profounder aspects of Hume's work and especially the Scottish naturalism which is its base, this is not due to any lack on his part of intelligence or industry. The fault lies with the spectacles on his nose. They turn everything into the positivism or empiricism with which they are tinted.

The point may be illustrated by reference to the work of a distinguished Hume scholar. David Fate Norton's book on Hume is valuable for the attention he gives to the intellectual background and especially to the Scottish naturalists.[16] He has an informative chapter, for example, on little known figures such as Turnbull and Kames. His view is that the naturalism of the Scottish school should be contrasted with that of Hume. The essential difference between the two is that the naturalism of the Scottish school is not thoroughgoing. Naturalists up to a point, they depend ultimately on their religious beliefs. Hence he refers to their view as providential naturalism or again as a 'curious supernatural naturalism'.[17] Thus they do not really hold that our natural beliefs are authoritative in themselves. They hold of course that they are true and must be accepted. But that is because 'they are convinced that our natural faculties are God-given, are a part of the overall design of a Providential nature, and can be trusted implicitly. They believe that what we naturally believe is in fact supernaturally guaranteed.'[18] In other words, the Scottish naturalists justify our natural beliefs by a belief in God. By contrast, no such appeal to God is found in Hume. Moreover, he has himself disproved the inference from the world to God's design, which is implicit in the naturalism of the Scottish school, by showing in the *Dialogues on Natural Religion* that any argument to design is valid only when it is derived from experience.

It may already be apparent that Norton views the Scottish naturalists on the basis of assumptions which belong to positivism or scientific naturalism. Thus, throughout his analysis, he treats their naturalism not as a doctrine in its own right but as a muddle-headed form of positivism. He refers to it, for example, as a curious supernatural naturalism. The view seems to him curious because he assumes that any clear-headed naturalism must be incompatible with a religious or supernatural view. But that is because he confuses *epistemological* naturalism, the view that our knowledge depends on what is given us by nature, with *metaphysical* naturalism, the view that there is no reality apart from the natural world. It is obvious that the former view does not entail the latter. Consequently there is no necessary incompatibility between naturalism and a religious or supernatural view. Norton thinks otherwise because he identifies every naturalism with the naturalism prevalent in our own culture.

Moreover, though this is the source it is not the sum of his misunderstandings. He holds, as we have seen, that the Scottish naturalists justify our natural beliefs by referring to the existence of God. Such is the force of preconception that he sustains this interpretation whilst repeatedly quoting passages from the Scottish naturalists which prove the exact opposite. Here, for example, is a passage which he quotes from Reid.

> The existence of a material world, and of what we perceive by our senses, is not self-evident according to (modern) philosophy. Descartes founded it upon this argument, that God, who hath given us our senses, is no deceiver, and therefore they are not fallacious. I endeavoured to show that, if it be not admitted as a first principle, that our faculties are not fallacious, nothing else can be admitted, and that it is impossible to prove this by argument, unless God should give us new faculties to sit in judgement upon the old.[19]

In this passage, it is plainly Descartes who attempts to justify our natural faculties by referring to the existence of God. Reid's view is precisely that this is misguided in principle. The authority of our natural faculties cannot be established by argument, for if they have no authority we have no reason to accept any argument. We could justify our faculties in that fashion only if God supplied us with entirely different faculties; only, in short, if we were transformed into entirely different creatures. In this passage, Reid plainly rejects the very view that Norton attributes to him. We may take another example. Norton quotes the following passage from Lord Kames.

> If I can only be conscious of what passes through my mind, and if I cannot trust my senses when they give me notice of external and independent existences; it follows, that I am the only being in the world; at least that I can have no evidence from my senses, of any other being, body or spirit. This is certainly an unwary concession, because it deprives us of our chief or only means for attaining knowledge of Deity.[20]

In this passage, Lord Kames clearly states that our knowledge of the Deity presupposes the authority of our natural belief in an independent world. Plainly, therefore, he cannot hold that the authority of this belief is founded on our knowledge of the Deity. One suspects that Norton misses the point in these passages because he takes for granted that one is not entitled to a belief unless one can justify it. In other words, he shares the empiricist assumption that every body of belief should rest on some form of rational justification.

But that is to miss the very essence of epistemological naturalism. For the Scottish naturalists, justification cannot arise unless we are *already* entitled to certain beliefs. As Reid says, the authority of our natural beliefs must be taken as a first principle. It is not itself justified because it is presupposed in all our justification. Thus our belief in God cannot be the *foundation* of our natural beliefs; it is only *through* our natural beliefs that we can come to a belief in God.

We may note finally, for it is tedious to multiply examples, that Norton's interpretation of the Scottish naturalists is especially ironic in the case of Hutcheson, who was prosecuted by the Presbytery of Glasgow for holding, amongst other things, 'that we could have a knowledge of good and evil, without, and prior to a knowledge of God'. The Scottish clergy no doubt had their faults, but, in this case at least, we may credit them with a clear understanding of the views they criticized.

What is true, as Norton illustrates, is that in developing their philosophy, the Scottish naturalists regularly gave expression to their religious views. But the most obvious reason for this is that they saw no incompatibility between the two. Indeed we may go further. Although religious views cannot *justify* natural belief, they may nevertheless serve to explain or render more *comprehensible* its authority. Assume that the world has a Creator and it is easy to explain that harmony between mind and nature which is exhibited in natural belief. Assume, by contrast, that the world is the product simply of chance or blind causation and that harmony becomes not easier to explain but altogether inexplicable. In this way, the religious views of the Scottish naturalists are not simply compatible with the philosophy of natural belief; in so far as they render the authority of natural belief more comprehensible, they serve to support it.

The above points are expressed by Reid himself, with his usual clarity, in the following passage, where he is discussing our belief in the authority of the senses.

> Shall we say, then, that this belief is the inspiration of the Almighty? I think this may be said in a good sense; for I take it to be the immediate effect of our constitution, which is the work of the Almighty. But if inspiration be understood to imply a persuasion of its coming from God, our belief of the objects of sense is not inspiration, for a man would believe his sense though he had no notion of a Deity. He who is persuaded that he is the workmanship of God and that it is a part of his constitution to believe his senses may think that a good reason to confirm his belief. But he had the belief before he could give this or another reason for it.[21]

Hume's philosophy, then, cannot be fully understood unless we recognize, first, that it contains incompatible elements and, second, that in its profounder elements it differs fundamentally from a later doctrine which superficially resembles it. Kemp Smith helps us to recognize the second point, but he does not sufficiently appreciate it himself; the first point he hardly appreciates at all. Therein lie the imperfections of his work. These imperfections are even more apparent in his celebrated introduction to Hume's *Dialogues on Natural Religion*. It is noticeable that his introduction to this work has been far more influential than his great study of Hume's whole philosophy. That is not surprising, for it conforms more closely to the assumptions of the culture. In his introduction, Kemp Smith argued that Hume, at least towards the end of his life, had come to accept what is effectively atheism and that the real aim of the *Dialogues* is to destroy the very essence of religious belief. There is some superficial evidence for this view in Hume's admiration for the enlightenment and in his antipathy to organized religion. It is unwise, however, to judge Hume's philosophical views by what he might wish to believe. It is one of his most remarkable qualities, the source of his greatness, that he will allow the philosophical argument to take him where he would not otherwise have wished to arrive. For example, he would have wished to accept the enlightenment ideal of reason. But in the *Treatise*, as Kemp Smith in effect argued, he entirely undermines that ideal. Indeed, as I shall show, in his view of the relation between reason and passion, he conforms much more closely to the Calvinism he detested than to the enlightenment he admired. In his introduction, Kemp Smith attempted a detailed defence of his interpretation of the *Dialogues*. The argument is tortuous, for he is too scrupulous a scholar to suppress any of the evidence. Unfortunately, the evidence, at numerous points, is plainly incompatible with his interpretation. The evidence is overwhelming that Hume never rid himself of his belief in God. Indeed it is evident that he never rid himself of his belief in the argument from design. For at the climax of the *Dialogues*, he affirms a version of precisely that argument.[22] His aim in the *Dialogues*, as I shall argue, is not to destroy but to limit the argument from design, and in particular to show that, so far as it is valid, it provides no support for organized religion. In a recent edition of the *Dialogues*, J. C. A. Gaskin reports the perplexity one of his colleagues experienced on first reading the work. He did not know where Hume stood. His perplexity is easy to understand, for it almost certainly arose from the incompatibility between what he knew to be the accepted view of the work and what he found when he actually read it. Kemp Smith is the person largely responsible for the accepted view.

The foregoing remarks provide us with our theme. It is the tension in Hume's philosophy between his empiricist inheritance and a certain kind of naturalism. To pursue that theme we must turn to a study of his most famous works, *The Treatise of Human Nature* and *The Dialogues Concerning Natural Religion*. Picking up this theme as it appears, we shall be guided through those works and may hope to obtain a clear view of Hume's philosophy as a whole.

2

AIMS AND METHODS IN THE
TREATISE

In his introduction to the *Treatise*, Hume deals with the nature of philosophy, its disorders and their cure. What he says is greatly influenced by the work of Newton. Indeed he argues that it is by following the method of Newton and by developing a science of human nature that the disorders of philosophy are to be cured. Unfortunately this view has been very widely misunderstood. It has been taken to mean that philosophy, when properly understood, is subservient to science and will flourish only when it adopts its method. In short, it has been seen as a commitment to positivism. But that is not at all what Hume meant. To appreciate this, one must realize that neither 'science' nor 'philosophy' meant for Hume what they mean for us. For us, 'science' means an activity which employs the categories and follows the procedures of the physical sciences, and especially mathematical physics. For Hume, 'science' and 'philosophy' were roughly interchangeable and meant any general form of study or learning. Thus physics was called natural philosophy, by which was meant the form of study which has as its object the natural or physical world. The terms, being used in so wide a sense, carry no commitment to any specific set of categories or type of procedure. Thus when Hume speaks in his introduction about a science of human nature, or of man, he in no way implies that this study will be committed to the categories or procedures of physical science. Indeed, as we shall see in a moment, he makes clear that this is impossible.

We may note further that the views which Hume expresses in his introduction are quite incompatible with positivism, at any rate in its developed form. Indeed the views expressed there strikingly resemble those of Kant. Thus, like Kant, Hume detects a disorder in philosophy. He finds its source, again like Kant, in the impulse to metaphysical speculation. To cure this impulse, we need a science of human nature. By this he means a study of human powers, which seeks as one of its principle aims to discern the *limits* of those powers. In short, to cure the disorder in philosophy, we must curb our desire to understand the world and must consider first what it is in the world that we are fitted to understand. We must turn back on ourselves. The method is precisely that of Kant.[1] When we thus turn back on ourselves we discern

15

the limits of our powers and discover also that speculative metaphysics is an abuse of those limits. We are now equipped to avoid problems of a speculative kind and to confine ourselves to those studies where we may reason to some profit. What we find here expressed is not a boundless confidence in the unlimited power of science. Quite the contrary; Hume's view is that science, by which he means any fruitful study of the world, is inevitably limited. And the point is to find its limits.

It is evident that what Hume meant by Newton's method is quite different from what the positivists meant by it. To clarify this, we must consider what Newton himself said. His remarks on method, which occur in the *Principia* and the *Opticks*, can be properly understood only when one takes into account the scientific disputes of his time. Thus his remarks in the General Scholium of the *Principia* are polemical in intent, being directed against the Cartesian view.[2] This is evident in itself, but is even more evident if one considers the preface which Roger Coates wrote for the second edition of the *Principia*. The point to grasp is that when he introduced gravitation into his system, Newton was in conflict with mechanical principles. On mechanical principles, causes operate only by impact and pressure; they are all, as is sometimes said, of the push and pull type. In attributing gravitational attraction to the particles of matter, Newton was attributing to them a force which cannot be explained in those terms. Both the strict atomists and the Cartesians criticized him on this ground. Their argument was that mechanical causation is already understood. Consequently it may be used as a principle of explanation. Gravitational attraction, which amounts to action at a distance, is not itself understood; indeed it is at least as difficult to understand as anything it may be used to explain. Thus Newton was accused of introducing into science one of those *occult* qualities so often ridiculed in the work of the scholastics. His famous remark 'I frame no hypotheses' was intended to rebut that charge.

The point may be clarified if for a moment we consider the Cartesian view. According to Descartes, what appears as action at a distance must be explained by mechanical principles and these, in their turn, by reference to the essential nature of matter.[3] In this way, we produce explanations which are truly systematic. Any explanation of a particular material phenomenon is connected with others and these together form a system based on the nature of matter itself. By contrast Newton's procedure is arbitrary, particular phenomena being explained by principles not themselves explained. Thus Descartes begins by claiming that the essence of matter lies in bare extension. Extension is continuous, allowing no gaps. The atom he explains as a vortex in continuous matter. One atom or vortex can affect another, at a distance, through the vibrations which run along the matter which is continuous between them. He adopted a similar explanation with regard to the system of the planets.

Now let us see how Newton's view differs from that of Descartes. His immediate objection is that if Descartes' views were true, they would not simply explain phenomena in a manner satisfactory to ourselves, they would have consequences which might be tested by observation. In fact, the consequences which ought to follow, were the views true, cannot be observed, and what can be observed is in conflict with the views themselves. Consequently, they should be rejected, *however consistent and satisfactory they might seem in themselves.* Moreover, should we find a principle that serves to explain phenomena and has consequences which can be confirmed in observation, then at least provisionally that principle should be accepted, *however unsatisfying or inexplicable it might otherwise seem.* This is what Newton meant by saying that he framed no hypotheses. The remark, as we shall see, has been taken in ways that he never intended. It must be understood in its context. What it means there is that his idea of a correct explanation in science is not determined by any preconceived view about the ultimate nature of matter. He calls this hypothesis or speculation. He deals not with matter in its ultimate nature but with material phenomena, *with matter as it appears to us.* It is this which determines what counts as a correct explanation. A correct explanation is what is forced on us in our attempt to explain material *phenomena.* Thus he introduces gravitational attraction, not because he understands its nature, but because he is convinced that the phenomena cannot be explained in any other way. He does not deny that questions can be raised about the nature of gravitation. *His point is that these are other questions.* They are not the questions he was seeking to answer when he introduced it in the first place.

Newton differs from Descartes as much in his conception of science as in his particular scientific views. Descartes' conception is suggested by mathematics. Thus in the study of a geometrical figure, such as the triangle, we begin with a definition of its essential nature and then proceed to features of a more particular kind, such as that the sum of its angles is equal to 180°. In a similar way, Descartes wishes to begin with the essence of matter and on this basis proceed to explain its particular features. Newton's point is that this misconceives the method of physical science. We cannot begin with the essence of matter, for it is not disclosed. We can begin only with matter as it appears to us, with material phenomena, which do not reveal their ultimate nature. In consequence physics, though it must be rigorous, cannot in Descartes' sense be systematic. For we possess no total system. We possess only the fragments of such a system, in matter as it appears to us. Consequently *any* explanation in physics must leave something *unexplained.* For matter appears to us only in part and therefore affords only particular explanations. Now we may certainly imagine that through a succession of partial explanations we shall arrive eventually at a *complete* account of the universe. But let us note, first, that this is merely an ideal and, second, that it is without definite content. For we do not know what categories it will contain. Indeed if we knew those categories we should already in its essentials possess such an account.

Now what we have just described *is* Newton's method. It consists in recognizing the limitations of the physical sciences which cannot grasp ultimate causes but must proceed by following the phenomena. As we shall see, Hume believes that there is a disorder in philosophy because philosophers have not followed this method. Their procedure is akin to Descartes'; they attempt, straight off, to grasp ultimate causes. The result is metaphysical speculation, not fruitful study. It may be noted that in recommending that philosophers adopt Newton's method, Hume is in no way suggesting that they should assume the procedure and concepts peculiar to mathematical physics. Indeed, as I have said, he makes clear in this very introduction that this is impossible.

> When I am at a loss to know the effects of one body upon another in any situation, I need only put them in that situation and observe what results from it. But should I endeavour to clear up after the same manner any doubt in moral philosophy, by placing myself in the same case with that which I consider, 'tis evident this reflection and premeditation would so disturb the operation of my natural principles, as must render it impossible to form any just conclusion from the phenomenon. We must therefore glean up our experiments in this science from a cautious observation of human life, and take them as they appear in the common course of the world, by men's behaviour in company, in affairs, and in their pleasures.[4]

It will be noted in the above passage that Hume's use of the term 'experiment' is as broad as his use of the term 'science'. For us, an experiment means an attempt to test an hypothesis by reproducing the relevant factors in a closed environment such as a laboratory. It is evident that this is not what Hume means by an experiment in the moral sciences for his whole point is that in the moral sciences this cannot be done. What he means by 'experiment' is simply putting to the test or checking against the facts. Thus the procedure he describes in the above passage is evidently more suited, for example, to the historian than to the physical scientist. The point he is making is one often made by those who oppose a unitary view of science. The procedures of the sciences should be appropriate to their subject matter and since they vary in their subject matter they require different procedures.

Before turning to the details of Hume's introduction, we must consider two points which arise from the above discussion. The first concerns the transformation of Newton's method in the hands of the positivists. In its earlier stages, positivism accepted Newton's distinction between matter in its ultimate nature and matter as it appears to us, arguing that science must confine itself to the phenomenal. In the course of the nineteenth century, however, physical science acquired an enormous prestige and its categories became treated as at least approximately *complete*. In consequence, matter in its ultimate nature was assumed to differ only in degree from matter as it appears, so that in time it would be explicable by categories already familiar to us. The effect of this is entirely to obliterate Newton's distinction. So strong has been the grip of this view on Western culture that it has continued to flourish in the present century, even though the categories of nineteenth-century science have been abandoned, being replaced by ones which differ from them not in degree but in kind. The view is merely transferred to the new categories which are thus treated, once again, as being approximately complete. It is important to note, however, that Hume is entirely free from this attitude.

The second point concerns Newton's use of the term hypothesis. His famous remark, as we have seen, needs to be taken in context. It is then evident that by an hypothesis he means some speculation about ultimate causes. It is in this sense that he denies that he frames hypotheses. He has often been assumed to deny, however, that scientific explanation involves *any* element of the hypothetical. On this assumption, science proceeds entirely through the accumulation of experiences. Thus we frame the law that dark clouds produce rain, because we have repeatedly experienced rain being produced by dark clouds. This process, which may be termed simple induction, has often been claimed to be the only legitimate scientific procedure. It is certain, however, that this is false. Indeed we may illustrate the point by reference to Newton's own procedure. His law of universal gravitation is based on Kepler's laws, which are based in their turn on Tycho Brache's observations. On the assumption we are considering, Kepler's laws would be obtained as a generalization of Brache's observations and Newton's law in a generalization of Kepler's. In fact, Kepler's laws, as Pierre Duhem showed, are consistent with any number of laws at a higher level so that Newton's law cannot be obtained from them simply as a generalization.[5]

We must distinguish between how a scientific law or theory arises and how it is verified. To verify a theory we rely on induction or repeated observations. It does not follow that repeated observations automatically *give rise* to a theory. The point is evident where a problem at the phenomenal or observational level can be removed only by referring to what lies below that level. The atomic theory is an obvious example. In this case, the theory evidently cannot be obtained simply from observation since what it refers to is not observable. What is observable are the consequences of the theory, which may serve to verify it. But that can occur only after the theory has arisen and it has arisen as a *conjecture* or *hypothesis* calculated to remove our problem. Indeed even in verifying or falsifying a theory, as Duhem also showed, we never find that observation is *coercive*. For an observation, however repeated, can always be interpreted differently by different theories.

Now from the above assumption, Hume was certainly *not* free. Indeed he enthusiastically embraced it. Throughout his work he assumes that scientific law or theory *arises* from induction or repeated observation. This had the effect of reinforcing the empiricist elements in his thought. It also had a disastrous effect on his philosophy of religion. In the *Dialogues*, for example, he assumes that any explanation of one event by another is impossible unless we have already had repeated experience of both. In this way, it is easy to lay waste to the whole of natural theology. Unfortunately, one lays waste also to the whole of theoretical science.

The introduction

Hume begins by stating that philosophy or metaphysics is in an unsatisfactory state. 'There is nothing which is not the subject of debate, and in which men of learning are not of contrary opinions.' 'Disputes are multiplied, as if everything was uncertain, and these disputes are managed with the greatest warmth, as if everything was certain.' In short, on any ultimate question, every philosopher has an opinion but it differs from that of almost every other philosopher. This has the consequence of bringing the subject into disrepute.

> From hence in my opinion arises that common prejudice against metaphysical reasonings of all kinds, even amongst those, who profess themselves scholars, and have a just value for every other part of literature. By metaphysical reasonings, they do not understand those on any particular branch of science, but every kind of argument, which is in any way abstruse, and requires some attention to be comprehended. We have so often lost our labour in such researches, that we commonly reject them without hesitation, and resolve, if we must for ever be a prey to errors and delusions, that they shall at least be natural and entertaining.[6]

Hume now considers what is to be done about this state of affairs. His view is that we should turn away from abstruse problems and consider what we can best understand, namely our own nature. Human nature, he says, is related in some manner to all the sciences.

> Even mathematics, natural philosophy and natural religion, are in some measure dependent on the science of man; since they lie under the cognizance of man, and are judged by their powers and faculties. 'Tis impossible to tell what changes and improvements we might make in these sciences were we thoroughly acquainted with the extent and force of human understanding and could explain the nature of the ideas we employ, and of the operations we perform in our reasonings.[7]

Hume now makes a comparison with recent developments in physics or natural philosophy. Great improvements have been made in that subject since scientists have abandoned the search for ultimate causes and have confined themselves to what can be discovered in phenomena through experience and observation. Comparable improvements can be expected in the science of man.

> Nor ought we to think, that this latter improvement in the science of man will do less honour to our native country than the former in natural philosophy, but ought rather to esteem it a greater glory, upon account of the greater importance of that science, as well as the necessity it lay under of such a reformation. For to me it seems evident, that the essence of the mind, being equally unknown to us with that of external bodies, it must be equally impossible to form any notion of its powers and qualities otherwise than from careful and exact experiments, and the observation of those particular effects, which result from its different circumstances and situations. And tho' we must endeavour to render all our principles as universal as possible, by tracing up our experiments to the utmost, and explaining all effects from the simplest and fewest causes, 'tis still certain we cannot go beyond experience; and any hypothesis, that pretends to discover the ultimate original qualities of human nature, ought at first to be rejected as presumptuous and chimerical.[8]

We may note here how closely Hume follows Newton's method. The essence of mind, like that of matter, is unknown. Consequently we must reject at first as presumptuous and chimerical any attempt to determine its ultimate principles. Rather we must proceed from mental phenomena as they appear in ordinary circumstances, attempting so far as possible to arrive at general conclusions but not supposing that we are in possession of a complete system.

In this respect, it is important to consider Hume's remark "'tis still certain we cannot go beyond experience'. Amongst later philosophers that would be taken as a logical remark to the effect that beyond experience there is nowhere one can conceivably go. In short, there is nothing which will not be known, at least in principle, through human experience. But that is not at all what Hume means. In him, the remark acknowledges an inevitable limit. Human experience is inevitably limited because in its fundamental nature the world transcends it. We must distinguish a sphere in which the world appears to human experience and one in which it transcends that experience. It is the part of wisdom to have a sense of the difference between the two spheres, so that it does not waste itself in pursuing what surpasses it but may confine itself to what is fruitful. That is precisely what Hume recommends.

It may already be noted that the benefits which Hume takes to accrue from a science of man are both positive and negative. Thus on the one hand we may expect an increase in our positive knowledge of human nature. We may note here, incidentally, a further respect in which Hume differs from later philosophers. As is evident in the first sentence of the last quotation, Hume takes for granted that a knowledge of human nature is bound to be more important and valuable to human beings than any knowledge about the physical world. But on the other hand we may expect an increased understanding of what we *cannot* know, a better knowledge, in short, of our limitations. With regard to the disorder in philosophy, it is this knowledge which is the more important. The point is evident in the following passage.

> For nothing is more certain, than that despair has almost the same effect upon us with enjoyment, and that we are no sooner acquainted with the impossibility of satisfying any desire, than the desire itself vanishes. When we see, that we have arrived at the utmost extent of human reason, we sit down contented; 'tho we be perfectly satisfied in the main of our ignorance, and perceive that we can give no reason for our most general and most refined principles, besides our experience of their reality; which is the reason of the mere vulgar, and what it required no study at first to have discovered for the most particular and most extraordinary phenomenon. And as this impossibility of making any further progress is enough to satisfy the reader, so the writer may desire a more delicate satisfaction from the free confession of his ignorance, and from his prudence in avoiding that error, into which so many have fallen, of imposing their conjectures and hypotheses on the world for the most certain principles. When this mutual contentment and satisfaction can be obtained betwixt the master and scholar, I know not what more we can require of our philosophy.[9]

Metaphysical curiosity can be assuaged only by understanding that it cannot be satisfied and that understanding can be acquired only through the science or study of human powers. For that study will show the limits of human powers and thereby bring an end to metaphysical speculation. In so doing, it will also cure the disorder in philosophy.

Hume goes only thus far in his introduction. But he already hints at how he will develop his theme. His theme will be that the limits of reason are necessary not accidental, because reason depends for its cogency precisely on those limits. There is a hint of this in the above passage where Hume suggests that we have no reason for our most general or refined principles, though we can experience their reality. Reason depends for its power on its relation to our other faculties and to those attitudes or beliefs which are implicit in their exercise. In short, it is fruitful only in relation to principles *not themselves based on reason*. It is properly an instrument which depends for its control, and therefore proper use, on other faculties and principles.

There is, however, a difficulty. For how then are we to account for metaphysics? The characteristic of metaphysics is that reason engages in *limitless* speculation. How is this possible if reason is properly an instrument, subordinate to other faculties and principles? The answer is that metaphysics is a *disorder* of reason. It is disordered just so far as it is limitless, for order implies limits. Metaphysics arises through an excess of force in reason which drives it beyond its natural limits or proper function. Hence we find the usual features of metaphysical speculation, the raising of questions that admit of only arbitrary solution, the proliferation of systems, the inability to find agreement. These are signs of disorder, of apparent power and real impotence. As a recoil there arises philosophical scepticism, the disparagement of reason in all its operations, which is a symptom of the same disorder. Reason is properly a practical not a metaphysical instrument. In turning metaphysical, it turns against its proper function. It is the aim of a sound philosophy to elucidate that function, thereby eliminating both metaphysical speculation and philosophical scepticism. Here we have what is essentially the theme of the *Treatise*.

3

EMPIRICIST ASSUMPTIONS

It will be noted that Hume, in his introduction, conforms very closely to the central views of Scottish naturalism. This is especially evident in his claim that we have no reason for our most general and refined principles. We must now consider how he is hampered in the development of his naturalism by accepting many of the empiricist assumptions which were common amongst his contemporaries. These assumptions are apparent in the opening chapters of the *Treatise*.

Hume, at the beginning of his work, divides the perceptions of the human mind into two kinds, which he calls impressions and ideas. He distinguishes between the two in terms of force and liveliness. When I see an object, I have a vivid impression of it. When the impression ceases, I am left with an idea or image, fainter than the impression, which copies it. In that way, I can think of the impression when I no longer have it.

We may note that Hume is here explaining perception in terms which seem entirely mechanical. Perception is a process in which the world impresses itself on the mind rather than one in which the mind is active in discriminating what is in the world. We may note also that the perceiver is a spectator rather than an agent. The point will be more evident as we proceed, but Hume tends to treat perception in abstraction from the perceiver's wider activities. It is as though in perception we merely register what is before us rather than discriminate its features in pursuit of our interests or purposes. For that reason, Hume is forced to distinguish between impressions and ideas, perceiving and thinking, not in terms of their wider roles but by means of internal features, their force or vivacity. This means that he has already accepted assumptions which will work against his naturalism, for this demands that the workings of the mind be elucidated precisely by reference to those wider relations with the world. He assumes, by contrast, that our grasp of the world arises through its reflection in our minds. But these are points to which we shall return.

Having distinguished between impressions and ideas, Hume makes a further division amongst them, between those which are simple and those which are complex. A complex impression or idea is made up of simple ones.

Thus an impression of colour is simple, but the impression of an apple is complex, since it consists of a number of impressions, such as those of colour, taste and smell. Hume says that a simple idea is the copy of a simple impression, there being nothing in the idea which was not in the impression. The same is not quite true of the relation between impressions and ideas, where our ideas are complex. There are complex ideas which have no corresponding complex impressions. That is because complex ideas can be compounded in the imagination, as when I frame the idea of a unicorn. Later, Hume will argue that when the imagination compounds ideas, it works according to certain principles which he calls the principles of association. For the moment, however, he emphasizes that although there may be nothing which corresponds to a complex idea as such, there will always be something which corresponds to each of the ideas out of which it is compounded. Thus every complex idea is compounded of simple ones and every simple idea has a simple impression corresponding to it. Hume's view, in other words, is that the imagination never creates anything which is absolutely new. It merely rearranges material which is supplied by the impressions.

But Hume now introduces a further distinction, the full significance of which becomes apparent only later. He distinguishes amongst impressions between those of sensation and those of reflection. The impression, say, of a bull may give rise in me to an impression of fear. Moreover, if my impression of the bull is retained in my mind as an idea it may prolong or reactivate my impression of fear. The fear is an impression of reflection rather than of sensation, because it is not, as it were, given to me directly by the world. Rather it is my reaction to what the world gives me. For example, the farmer who owns the bull may have the same impression of the bull as I, but he need not react as I do with fear. The same point applies to impressions of desire and aversion, hope and despair, and so on. As Hume proceeds, the significance of this distinction becomes apparent. For it soon becomes clear that he is attributing our fundamental ideas and beliefs not to ideas of sensation but to those of *reflection*. In short, our fundamental ideas and beliefs are not simply impressed on us by sense experience. They arise through what we *contribute* to what is given us by sense experience. Unfortunately, Hume is so entangled in a mechanical model that he cannot develop the point in detail. Nevertheless it is clear what he is struggling towards. Contrary to what Kant himself thought, he was *not* original in supposing that there is an a priori, yet synthetic element in our knowledge of the world. He was anticipated by Hume and even more evidently by Reid.[1]

We have now given in outline the basic categories which Hume uses throughout his work. As I have implied, he took them as established and he sought to modify but not in any fundamental way to criticize them. In the remainder of Part I, he makes further discriminations amongst the various faculties of the mind and amongst different types of idea. It will be useful to consider some of his main points.

He proceeds first to distinguish between the ideas of the imagination and those of memory. The first difference between the two is in force or vivacity. According to Hume an idea of the imagination is less vivid than one of memory. The second is that ideas in the imagination, unlike those in memory, are not exact copies of what gives rise to them. He is here repeating his point that the imagination has a certain freedom in how it arranges its material. He goes on to argue, however, that this freedom is not absolute. There are laws or principles which govern the imagination in its workings. These are the so-called principles of association. The mind in reverie, for example, may seem at first to move quite freely from one image to another. Later, one can often trace a pattern in its movement, one image being linked to another through a resemblance or through a past experience. At the time of the *Treatise*, Hume placed a great deal of weight on these principles. He thought they had a role to play within his science of man which would be comparable with the role that the laws of nature play in physical science. Once again, however, it is important to appreciate what he meant by this. It must be remembered that he did not believe the laws of nature could provide an ultimate explanation of the universe. They formulated the workings of nature, so far as they fell within our experience. But he had no doubt that these workings had their causes, and those still further causes, the whole passing beyond our comprehension. It was in a similar light that he considered the laws of association. They revealed the mind in some of its workings, but those workings have their causes, which are unknown. In no way do the laws of association provide an ultimate explanation for the workings of the mind. The point is evident in the following passage.

> Here is a kind of Attraction, which in the mental world will be found to have as extraordinary effects as in the natural, and to show itself in as many and as various forms. Its effects are everywhere conspicuous; but as to its causes, they are mostly unknown, and must be resolved into *original* qualities of human nature, which I pretend not to explain. Nothing is more requisite for a true philosopher, than to restrain the impetuous desire of searching into causes, and having established any doctrine upon a sufficient number of experiments, rest contented with that, when he sees that a further examination would lead him into obscure and uncertain speculations. In that case his enquiry would be much better employed in examining the effects than the causes of his principles.[2]

Hume therefore rests content with formulating various ways in which association works. For example, where objects *resemble* one another, the idea of one may suggest the idea of the other; the same thing will occur where two objects are *contiguous* or connected by time and place; again, where two events are connected by *causality*, the idea of the cause will suggest the idea of the effect. It will be noted that association is *mechanical* in its workings, comparable in the mental sphere with gravitation in the physical, and that whilst Hume is quite free from the idea that mechanical categories are sufficient to explain the mind in the ultimate nature, he will nevertheless restrict himself to those categories for the purpose of his account. Here, once again, he restricts himself in the development of his naturalism. As we shall see, this constitutes the one really important difference between Hume and Kant in their account of causality. Hume recognizes that our knowledge of causality presupposes an a priori relation between our minds and the world. But he renders the point obscure, because in describing the workings of the mind he is forced to employ only mechanical terms.

Hume completes Part I of his book by considering our ideas of relations, modes and substances, and our abstract ideas. It will be useful to consider in some detail the last of these. By an abstract idea, Hume means a general one, not the idea of this red object but of red objects in general. Hume's account of the relation between impression and idea is at its most plausible when we consider a particular object. It is easy to suppose that the idea of this red object is a kind of image which arises in the mind through one's impression of the object. But how does one form an image of red objects in general? For example, red comes in different shades, from very dark red to very light. How can one form an image of red which is simultaneously light and dark? The difficulty seems even worse with the more general concept of colour itself. This covers red, green, yellow, and so on. How can one simultaneously form an image of all those colours? Moreover, if an idea is a kind of image and we cannot form a general image, we cannot form general or abstract ideas at all. How does Hume try to get out of this difficulty?

He tries to do so by adopting a view of Berkeley's. According to Berkeley, an idea becomes general by being made to represent or stand for all other particulars of the same sort. Hume develops this view by means of an analogy. Suppose someone is unable to recollect a song or a poem. Very often, if you give him the opening words or notes, the whole song or poem will come back to him. Particular words or notes have the capacity to call up others. Now similarly, if a child has been taught to apply the word red in a number of cases, the word in other circumstances will itself call up appropriate instances. In short, the child does not have to carry all the instances simultaneously in his or her head. They will come readily enough when they are needed. Thus, on Hume's account, a general idea is a particular image which has acquired a representative capacity.

It is certain, however, that this account is defective. To see this, note that if a child is able, on the basis of an image, to recall instances of the appropriate kind, he or she must *already* have some ability to distinguish the kind. The child must know what other instances fall into the same kind as the image in his or her mind. But then this knowledge or ability cannot be explained by that image. The explanation runs the other way. The image acquires a general or representative function through its stimulating the child's ability to distinguish the kind. Indeed it is obvious that if an image acquires generality through its representative function, the generality lies in the function not in the image itself. Further reflection will reveal that the image is redundant. Suppose a child learns the use of 'red' so that he or she is able to pick out red objects in the same way as everyone else. Then we are satisfied that the child has the general idea of red, whatever image may come into his or her mind. The point is the more obvious in that some people do not have mental imagery, yet they can master general ideas. The point is that a general idea is not an entity; rather it is a capacity. One grasps ideas so far as one acquires the capacity to handle signs. Grasping a sign is not something that happens in the head. It is more like grasping the use of an instrument, which involves its exercise in relation to the world more generally.

We may note further that the generality which is involved in our capacity to handle signs is not acquired through experience but is inherent in the workings of the mind. Indeed if it were not thus inherent, nothing could be acquired by experience. The point is evident in the case of the animals. A dog does not acquire the capacity to distinguish its food through trial and error in innumerable particular cases. It would be dead before it acquired the capacity. It already has a capacity to distinguish what kind of food will nourish it and in particular cases looks for instances of the kind. The general precedes the particular. We may note, also, that the animal's capacity reveals a relation to the world which is functional not mechanical. Thus the dog is so related to the world that it can distinguish within it what will keep it alive. Further, in detecting its food, in a particular instance, the dog is not simply registering what is there but is actively discriminating in pursuit of its purposes or interests.

Now, on an empiricist account such as Hume's, the particular precedes the general. One arrives at complex ideas by compounding simple ones. If one reflects for a moment, however, one will see that the generality involved in an abstract idea is irreducible to any set of particular cases. Thus one may certainly refer to particular cases in teaching children, say, the concept of red. But they have acquired the concept only when they *go beyond* the cases used in teaching them, only when they apply the term red, quite independently, *to others of the kind*. Moreover, in speaking about others of the kind we do not refer to any finite set of cases, however numerous. It is precisely that the child's use of the term is no longer confined to a finite set which shows he or she has mastered it. The child can now pick out not simply what happens to be red, but *whatever* is red. He or she can go on *indefinitely*.

Moreover, the child's knowledge does not begin with sharp particulars moving later to generalities, equally sharp. It begins in vague generalities. That is why, for example, a child is liable at first to call almost any man father. Only later does he or she fix on the particular man. Oddly enough, Hume himself provides an example which illustrates the point. The idea of colour is obviously distinct from that of a shape. But one cannot have an image of the one without having the image of the other. You cannot have the image of a colour without its having a shape, or the image of a shape without its having a colour. How then do you distinguish between the two? You cannot do so on the basis of a particular image. You need already to have grasped the distinction in general. Thus if you see a round white object, you can distinguish the shape from the colour only because you have seen round objects which are not white and white objects which are not round. Moreover, even that is not sufficient. You need to bring this knowledge to bear on the particular case. In short you can distinguish *a particular* colour from its shape only because you have the idea of shape and colour *in general*.

That shows, once again, that an idea is not an image. An image is ambiguous and needs to be interpreted. Thus if you could look into a person's mind and see what images were occurring there, you still could not tell what that person is thinking. Suppose you can see that in my mind I have an image of a round white object. You cannot tell whether I am thinking of its shape or of its colour. You need to know my relations to the world more generally. For example, you need to know what was occurring before I had the image and what I go on to say or do later.

It is evident that Hume's empiricist account is ill-equipped to elucidate the idea of generality. One reason is that it construes the mind in quasi-physical terms. It will already be evident, for example, that Hume treats an idea as a kind of object, differing from a physical object only in that it occurs in the mind. Moreover, that is not the only difficulty. The very phrase 'in the mind' suggests another. To see the point, consider a mental activity such as reading. One may read either aloud or silently. If one reads silently, one may be said to be reading *in one's mind*. Here the phrase makes a contrast with what occurs in public. Now the empiricist reduces the mental to what is in the mind, *in that sense*. In short, he dissociates the mental from the public realm and associates it with the private. Thus on an empiricist view, the process of reading would be essentially in the mind. Reading aloud would be the outward expression of what is occurring in private. In fact, this is the reverse of the truth. Reading aloud is the primary activity for that is how everyone learns to read. Indeed for some centuries no one read in any other way; everyone read aloud. In other words, silent reading is a later acquisition which is parasitic on reading in the public realm. Similar points apply to meaning. On the empiricist view, an idea is an image, which occurs 'in the mind'. Only later do we give it outward expression in language. The process evidently runs the other way. Certainly I can think to myself, without expressing my thoughts; but then I have already learned to express myself in language. It is difficult to see how there could be a coherent alternative. If meaning is essentially private, I cannot know what you tell me until I know what is in your mind. But in innumerable cases, I cannot know what is in your mind until you tell me. On this account, language would be impossible.

29

Here we return to a point which was mentioned at the beginning of this chapter. Hume treats impressions and ideas, the workings of the mind, in abstraction from our active engagement with the world. But it will be apparent on reflection that the powers or capacities of the mind must evidently reveal themselves precisely in that engagement. The result is that Hume is forced to ignore or distort those powers or capacities. It will be useful to give a final illustration. Hume treats memory as the present occurrence in the mind of an image which copies a past impression. So far we have a mechanical process, hardly distinguishable from what occurs in a camera. Thus in a camera there is a present image which copies an event earlier impressed on it. So far we have nothing distinctive of memory. For what is distinctive of memory is not that a past event has produced in me a present occurrence but that in the present occurrence I am *aware* of the past event. In short, so far as we confine ourselves to the mechanical, we do not find memory. Finding memory, we find also that we have left the mechanical and are dealing with the *intentional*. Thus a memory image is an image *of* the past event; otherwise it does not belong to the memory. But the word 'of' signifies an intentional relation. It means that the image *refers* to the past event. How then is this reference to be understood? Certainly not in terms of copying, for that occurs in a camera which of itself makes no reference. Moreover, unless I am *already* aware of the past event how do I know that my present image copies it? I cannot compare it with my past impression, for that no longer exists. It is evident that the mechanical process, which Hume describes, can lead on to memory only if it is supplemented by a mental capacity which cannot be explained in mechanical terms. Certainly we are so related to the world that we can be aware not simply of what is occurring but also of what has already occurred. But that is a capacity which can be identified neither with an 'impression' nor with an 'idea'. In short, it fits into neither of Hume's basic categories.

The consequences of empiricism

The above criticisms of Hume's empiricist views are intended to show not simply that they are inadequate in themselves but that they are inadequate to support a naturalism of the Scottish type. Thus, on the naturalist view, our knowledge has its source not in our own sense experience or reasoning but in general capacities given to us by nature. For that reason those capacities must be elucidated in their relation to the world more generally and must be shown in their workings to be intentional or purposive, not mechanical. All these features are obliterated in the empiricist account. It treats all our faculties and capacities as subordinate to sense experience and reasoning; it confines the mind to a private realm and treats its workings as mechanical. The two accounts are incompatible and any philosophy which attempts to combine both will involve itself in irreconcilable conflict.

Now after a brief and unsatisfactory section on our ideas of space and time, Hume in the remainder of Part I considers three of the ideas that are fundamental in all our thought. He begins with our idea of causality, to which we shall turn in the next chapter. He then proceeds to consider our ideas of an independent world and of the self, and at the same time discusses the nature of philosophical scepticism. Throughout, his *aim* is clear. He seeks to show that these ideas are not derived from any insight into the objective processes of nature. They arise rather from certain processes which are instinctive or natural to the mind. For example, our idea of causality arises from our instinctive relation to regularity. But regularity is not the same as causality. Consequently, though we believe in causality, though indeed it is fundamental to all our knowledge, we cannot explain or justify what we believe. The point is *not* that we are unreasonable to hold that belief. The point is that such a belief is presupposed in what we treat as reasonable or unreasonable. Reason, indeed, depends on such a belief for its power or cogency. In consequence, it cannot undermine the belief without undermining itself. Hence there is in philosophical scepticism an evident absurdity, for it seeks in the name of reason to undermine the beliefs or principles on which reason itself depends. Moreover, we now see clearly that reason is not a metaphysical instrument, since it depends for its power on beliefs or principles it has not itself established.

The aim is clear. The difficulty is in the execution. To establish his view, Hume needs to show how those ideas arise, independently of rational insight, through the instinctive or natural workings of the mind. But he is so entangled in empiricist assumptions that he cannot give a plausible account of those workings. Thus at certain points we are plunged into the very scepticism which he seeks to remove. The difficulty is not equally great in every case. With the exercise of some charity, we can remove the empiricist elements from his account of causality, leaving that account both consistent and powerful. It is an altogether different matter to rescue his account of how we arrive at the idea of an independent world. Hume gives an account of this, on the basis of material which is entirely private or subjective. On the basis of such material, one cannot make the idea intelligible, much less show how it arises.[3]

But these are matters to which we must now turn, in detail, beginning with Hume's famous account of causality.

4

CAUSATION

Hume's analysis of causality in the *Treatise* contains a number of digressions, which sometimes make it difficult to follow his argument. We shall confine ourselves to its essential structure.

> To begin regularly [he says] we must consider the idea of *causation*, and see from what origin it is derived. 'Tis impossible to reason justly, without understanding perfectly the idea concerning which we reason; and 'tis impossible perfectly to understand any idea, without tracing it up to its origin, and examining the primary impression, from which it arises.[1]

It is important to note that Hume proposes to consider the *idea* of causation, not causation itself. In other words, he proposes to analyse how causation appears to us, what we know about it, rather than to reveal hitherto unknown facts about its ultimate nature. He will practise what used to be called conceptual analysis. Thus his aim is to consider an instance of causality, such as one billiard ball's moving another, in order to determine the features on which the application of the concept is based.

Now when we reflect on an instance, two features are readily apparent. The first is contiguity. The one ball is moved on contact with the other. The second is succession. The movement of the first ball is prior to the movement of the second. But these features, though necessary, are not sufficient to determine a causal relation.

> An object may be contiguous and prior to another, without being considered as its cause. There is a *necessary connexion* to be taken into consideration; and that is of much greater importance, than any of the other two above-mentioned.[2]

The important relation in causal succession is not one that falls beneath our eyes. Rather it is a relation, as it were, to the future. Thus we should never call a succession causal unless we were certain that in the appropriate circumstances it would *always* happen that way. It is not one billiard ball's moving another which makes us call the relation causal; it is our certainty that this was *bound* to happen and therefore always will. The question is precisely how this certainty can be based on what does fall beneath our eyes. How on the basis of a particular contiguous succession can we determine what will always happen? Where, in short, is the *necessity* in the relation?

Further reflection reveals a third feature. It is only rarely that we should call a succession causal on the basis of a single instance. Most often it is only when we have observed the succession occur a number of times that we treat it as causal. Here, then, we have a further feature, namely, constant conjunction. It seems evident, however, that constant conjunction, being mere repetition, cannot produce any new relation. What occurs on the tenth instance of a succession is only what occurred on the first. But, then, what we failed to find on the first occurrence cannot be found on the tenth. Constant conjunction, in short, cannot be identical with causality.

As we have seen, the above view is often denied. Many philosophers hold that for Hume causality is identical with constant conjunction. It is worth emphasizing therefore that their view is not simply in conflict with Hume's own words but makes nonsense of his whole analysis. Thus if he thought that causality is identical with constant conjunction, he would at this point have completed his analysis. He would have found what he seeks. It is obvious, however, that his inquiry is still in its preliminary stages.

Nevertheless, though constant conjunction is not identical with causality, it plays an important part in causal inference. If two events have been constantly conjoined in my experience, on seeing the one I frequently infer the other. We must inquire further into the nature of this transition. Why do I infer the one from the other, given that they have been conjoined in my experience? Hume now proceeds to make two related points. The first is that in inferring the one from the other, we take a step *beyond* our experience of their constant conjunction. The second is that this step is not itself based on reason.

It is easy to see that in causal inference we step beyond experience, for causal inference is concerned with the future. If I say that the first ball will move the second, I state not what *has* occurred but what *will* occur. What will occur, being in the future, lies as yet beyond my experience.

The question is whether this step is based on reason. Hume states first that it is not based on reason, in the sense of pure logic. For there is no *contradiction* in denying that the future will conform to the past. However often the first ball has moved the second, I do not contradict myself in saying that this time the second will not move.

But might not the step be based on a rational assessment of probability? Is it not highly probable, in all reason, that the second ball will move? Hume now shows that probable reasoning presupposes that the future will be like the past, which is just what it was supposed to establish. If we set aside logical demonstration, we are left with reasoning about matters of fact. But all reasoning about matters of fact presupposes the inference from cause to effect and therefore cannot establish it.

It is evident that constant conjunction will not give us what we seek. What we seek is necessity. Why are we certain that in the appropriate circumstances the second ball will *always* move? Neither through direct experience, nor yet through inference, can we get from constant conjunction the element we seek. But can reason and experience give us no better notion of causality than that of constant conjunction? May we not penetrate more deeply into the objective process and discover why events are constantly conjoined? Hume is adamant that this is impossible. The ultimate nature of causality is unknown.

> We have no notion of cause and effect, but that of certain objects which have been always conjoined together, and which in all past instances have been found inseparable. We cannot penetrate into the reason of the conjunction.[3]

Hence he concludes:

> Thus not only our reason fails us in the discovery of the *ultimate connexion* of causes and effects, but even after experience has informed us of their *constant conjunction*, 'tis impossible for us to satisfy ourselves by our reason, why we shou'd extend that experience beyond those particular instances, which have fallen under our observation.[4]

This concludes the first part of Hume's analysis. It is entirely negative. If we confine ourselves to what reason and experience can reveal in the objective process, we cannot find what is most essential to our idea of causality. In short, this idea is not the product of a rational insight into the objective process.

But that is only the first part of the analysis. A second part awaits us. So far, we have supposed that the connection between causal inference and constant conjunction must depend on our own experience and reasoning. We have supposed, for example, that if we are certain, on the basis of past experience, that the second ball will move, we must have grasped some *reason* why on the basis of past experience we should be certain. We have supposed, in Hume's vocabulary, that causal inference is based on a *philosophical* relation. By a philosophical relation he means one which is grasped through reasoning or reflection. Constant conjunction is a philosophical relation. To know that a succession has occurred a number of times one must reflect on one's past experiences. But in addition to philosophical relations there are natural ones. In short, there are relations between the mind and the world which are prior to reasoning or reflection. Now so far as we confine ourselves to philosophical relations we find nothing in causality but contiguity, succession and constant conjunction. These are *insufficient* to explain the inference from cause to effect. What Hume suggests, however, is that this inference depends on processes he calls natural.

> Thus tho' causation be a *philosophical* relation, as implying contiguity, succession, and constant conjunction, yet 'tis only so far as it is a *natural* relation and produces an union among our ideas, that we are able to reason upon it, or draw any inference from it.[5]

Hume here gives a clue to his positive analysis. What he is suggesting is that there is a relation between causation and the mind, a relation not based on reasoning but one on which reasoning itself depends. To appreciate his point, we must recall that if we could not infer from cause to effect we could not reason about the world at all. Now what enables us to reason about the world cannot itself be the product of our reasoning. Unless we were already fitted to reason about the world, we could not have done so in the first place. Our very existence depends on our certainty about cause and effect. Nature has not trusted that to our fallible reasoning.

In his positive analysis, Hume will show how the idea of causality arises not through a philosophical relation but through workings which are instinctive or natural to the mind. This will not explain the nature of causation; it will explain how our certainty about causation does not depend on our understanding its nature.

Belief

Hume does not reveal the details of his final analysis until section XIV. In the meantime, he deals with a number of related issues. As I have said, we shall not follow him in this but shall confine ourselves to the essential structure of his argument. It will be useful nevertheless to touch on one of the issues he raises, because it is directly related to his final analysis and because it will enable us to illustrate how he is hampered by his empiricist assumptions in making his fundamental points. After making the points we have just discussed, he turns to consider the nature of belief. His strategy in doing so is fairly clear. His aim is to show that belief has its roots in the natural workings of the mind rather than in processes of reasoning, thereby supporting his suggestion that the same will prove true of our belief in causality. The difficulty is that in describing the workings of the mind, he is confined to the categories of impression, idea and association. Once again, we must emphasize that he does not believe these categories will *explain* the workings of the mind. What he believes is that they will enable him to give a description of the mind which is sufficient to show that processes of reasoning are not fundamental to its workings. The trouble is that his categories are so impoverished that they will not enable him to accomplish even this limited a task. To illustrate the point, let us consider what he says about belief.

Hume begins by arguing that to have the idea of existence comes to the same thing as having the idea of an object. To have the idea of an object is to have the idea of it *as* existing. But that creates an obvious difficulty. For how does one have the idea that an object does *not* exist? With regard to mathematical and logical ideas, the difficulty does not arise, since the contradictory of these ideas is inconceivable. But with regard to matters of fact, the difficulty obviously does arise. On any empirical issue, we can see both sides of the issue. We can entertain the idea of an object without committing ourselves to a belief in its existence. Hume's answer to this difficulty is that belief consists in the *manner* by which an idea is entertained. On the face of it, this is plausible. For example, of two people who have the idea that it is raining, one may be sure and the other unsure that it is true. They have the same idea. The difference seems to lie in the *manner* with which they conceive it.

There is a difficulty, however, in what Hume means by manner. Thus in the case of the two who differ over whether it is raining, we should expect their difference to show itself in what they have experienced previously, in what they would affirm, in what they go on to do, and so on. It would be difficult to give a precise list but we should expect any list to contain some such items. As we have seen, however, Hume considers the mind in abstraction from all such items, confining himself to what is severely *inner*. Consequently it is in such terms that he must describe the *manner* of conceiving an idea which constitutes belief. What he concludes is that the manner of conceiving an idea consists in the *force* or *vivacity* with which it is conceived. He seems here to be referring to vividness of imagery. The one who believes the idea is the one who more vividly conceives of it in his mind. But that is surely quite implausible. For example, the man who believes the idea may not conceive very vividly what it involves. Perhaps that is why he believes it. Someone who conceives of it more vividly can see that it is doubtful. Here it is the one who does not believe whose conception is the more vivid. It is possible, however, that Hume is referring not to vividness of imagery but to some feeling of confidence which accompanies belief. The trouble is that this is equally inadequate. In some contexts such feelings may be present; but in others they are quite absent. If you ask me my name, I tell you. So far as I am aware, I have no feelings at all, whether or not of confidence. Moreover, what makes a feeling one of *confidence*? Surely it cannot be characterized in terms of bare sensation. Most commonly it occurs where we have been attempting to accomplish some task. But here we move beyond the inner and, especially, introduce the categories of *purpose* or *intention*. It is evident, in short, that Hume's categories will not enable him to provide an adequate account of belief.

Given the inadequacy of these categories, however, Hume shows some ingenuity in developing his account. He argues that the force or vivacity of an idea depends on its relation to an impression. If I have an impression, I am left with a vivid idea, which means that I believe it. By contrast, if I am merely turning over an idea in my mind, it is not related to any impression.

Consequently it is less vivid, which means I do not believe it. We may note that this analysis depends for its plausibility on our tacitly translating it into ordinary terms. Thus we think of someone who has an impression as one who sees an object and is thereby related to it. By contrast, we think of one who merely turns over an idea in his mind as being less directly related to what surrounds him. In short, we tacitly distinguish between the two in terms of their relation to an independent world. What we forget is that on Hume's official view an impression is as subjective as an idea; it is something *inner*. But to continue with Hume's analysis, having related the vivacity of an idea to an impression, he now introduces the principles of association. If two impressions are often associated, there will be a similar association between their corresponding ideas. Thus if I have often seen it rain after having seen dark clouds, the sight of dark clouds will immediately suggest the idea of rain. Moreover, this idea, being so closely associated with an impression, will have the force or vivacity of belief. Now it may be noted that we have anticipated Hume's positive account of causal inference. He has given an account of how, on seeking dark clouds, we come to infer that it will rain. This account falls entirely within the categories of impression, idea and association. Moreover, it refers only to the natural or habitual workings of the mind. In other words, at no point in the account do we have to assume that the mind has any rational insight into the nature of causality as an objective process.

Unfortunately, it has grave weaknesses. Hume has committed himself to the view that we cannot infer one event from another until we have repeatedly experienced instances of both. Indeed, on his account, causal inference occurs quite mechanically through the mere accumulation of particular experiences. We have already noted the unfortunate effect this has on Hume's views in other areas of philosophy. For example, it falsifies his view of scientific explanation. But its weaknesses are evident, even if one simply considers ordinary circumstances. A young child, for example, is startled by a loud noise and instinctively turns towards its source. He has not found through repeated experience that noises this loud are startling and have a source he might turn towards. Again, a child feels a tug on something he holds. Instinctively he turns towards its cause. This again has not been learned through repeated experience. There are many other such cases. It is evident that nature in endowing us with the causal attitude does not have to work through the mechanism of repeated experiences. From the beginning the child has the causal attitude. It is true that we may consult experience on various occasions in order to select the appropriate cause. But we already have the idea of cause when we consult experience in order to select the appropriate one.

Before turning to the details of Hume's positive analysis, we must consider what weight to place on these weaknesses. To assess this, we must keep in mind Hume's main or essential thesis. His essential thesis is that our idea of causality arises through instinctive or natural workings of the mind and not through an insight into the objective process. The question is whether this thesis depends on his empiricist assumptions. It seems to me certain that this is not so. To remove those assumptions will be to strengthen rather than to weaken the thesis itself. Consider the child who reacts to the tug by turning to its cause. It is difficult to believe that the source of this reaction lies in repeated experience. But it is even more difficult to believe that it lies in a rational insight into the nature of causation. It seems evidently not to depend on reasoning at all. Moreover, to remove Hume's empiricist assumptions is not simply an exercise in charity. He himself supports his main thesis by a number of examples which do not at all depend on those assumptions. For example, he points out that the basis of causal inference already exists amongst the animals. From the tone of its master's voice, the dog anticipates his anger. From what it smells it knows that its game is not far away. Now it is irrelevant whether or not these reactions conform to empiricist assumptions. What is certain is that they do not rest on a rational insight into the nature of causation. The dog anticipates its game through what it smells, but that is not because it perceives a necessary connection between the two and then proceeds to react. Here it is manifest that what is fundamental is the natural reaction.

We must now turn to section XIV, where Hume completes his analysis.

The positive analysis

As we have already seen, Hume's account of causal inference will depend on his linking constant conjunction to the mechanism of association which underlies belief. Constant conjunction is therefore important to the account. It is important, however, not because it is identical with causality but because it sets going the processes of association. It is these processes which will give rise to the idea of causality. In short, that idea will arise not from what we see but from how we *react* to what we see. In Hume's vocabulary, it will arise not from an impression of sensation but from one of *reflection*. Thus it is not important in itself that I have seen two events constantly conjoined. What is important is that when I now see the one I immediately infer the other. The idea of causality arises therefore through a reaction to what I see. *More strictly*, it arises most immediately through a reaction to what I *do* when I see it. Thus I have repeatedly experienced one ball's moving another. On seeing the movement of the first, I am immediately determined to infer the movement of the second. *It is because I feel myself thus determined that I treat the process as a determined one.* Hume expresses the point in the following terms at the beginning of section XIV.

> For after a frequent repetition, I find, that upon the appearance of one of the objects, the mind is *determined* by custom to consider the usual attendant, and to consider it in a stronger light upon account of

its relation to the first object. 'Tis this impression, then, or *determination*, which affords me the idea of necessity.[6]

Earlier, Hume had given a hint of this view in the following terms. 'Perhaps 'twill appear in the end, that the necessary connexion depends on the inference, instead of the inference's depending on the necessary connexion.'[7]

In these terms we have what seems to me the most profound formulation of Hume's positive view. Our idea of necessity in the events arises not simply from what we see in those events but from the certainty with which we infer the one from the other. It is not because we see a necessity in the two events that we infer the one from the other; it is because we infer the one from the other that we treat them as necessary. It may be noted that Hume in effect has abandoned the categories of empiricism, for he appeals not to a private occurrence in the mind but to what we do, the way we react to an independent world. Thus it is not because the dog perceives a necessary connection between the two that it reacts to the smell by anticipating its game. What it does, the way it reacts, is more fundamental than any of its particular perceptions. Similarly, our idea of necessity in the world arises from relations between the world and ourselves which are more profound than any product of our own observation or explicit reasoning.

Having given at the beginning of section XIV the details of his own positive account, Hume now turns to those of other philosophers. He remarks that philosophers have readily engaged in disputes about causality without making even a preliminary inquiry into what we mean by causal power or necessity. 'But before they enter'd upon these disputes it would not have been improper to have examined what idea we have of that efficacy, which is the subject of the controversy.'[8]

Thus, on the Cartesian view, matter itself cannot give us an adequate idea of causal power. Consequently we must suppose that this power lies rather in God than in matter itself. Hume says that this view is irrelevant to his own inquiry, for granting that we have no adequate idea of the power in matter, we have no better idea of this power in God. Equally irrelevant is the view of those who attribute causal power to matter but claim that it lies in qualities that are unknown to us. Hume is not denying, it is important to note, that there may be such qualities.

> I am, indeed, ready to allow, that there may be several qualities both in material and immaterial objects, with which we are utterly unacquainted; and if we please to call them *power* or *efficacy*, 'twill be of little consequence to the world. But when, instead of meaning these unknown qualities, we make the terms of power and efficacy signify something of which we have a clear idea, and which is incompatible with those objects to which we apply it, obscurity and error begin then to take place, and we are led astray by a false philosophy.[9]

Hume is not concerned to deny that there are unknown properties in matter that would explain our treating the causal process as necessary.[10] His point is that a reference to those properties cannot explain how we acquired the idea of necessity in the first place. Indeed his criticism is graver than this, for he implies that these philosophers are not consistent in their usage. At one moment, they use 'causal power' to refer to unknown properties in the objective process, but at the next we find them speaking as though we had a clear or adequate idea of those very properties, hitherto said to be unknown. In this way, they convey an entirely spurious impression of our ability to understand the objective process. We shall return to the implications of this criticism.

Hume now returns to his own analysis, repeating its details and stating his conclusion. Here we shall note for the last time the intrusion into his account of his empiricist assumptions. Thus he states his conclusion as follows.

> Upon the whole, necessity is something that exists in the mind, not in objects; nor is it possible for us ever to form the most distant idea of it, considered as a quality in bodies. Either we have no idea of necessity, or necessity is nothing but that determination of the thought to pass from causes to effects, according to their experienced union.[11]

Taken strictly, this means that when we speak of two events as causally related, we are really speaking not about those events but about our own minds. And indeed this is what follows from his empiricist assumptions. For since every idea must copy an impression and since the idea that gives rise to necessity is an impression of reflection, of something in our minds, then the idea of that impression must also be an idea of what is in our minds. Consequently when we speak of events as causally related we are really speaking about what passes through our minds when we observe them. The trouble with this is that it is absurd and it requires little charity to restate Hume's views in terms which are not only acceptable in themselves but are faithful to his fundamental insight. It is true that when we speak of events as causally related we convey as much about ourselves as about the events. For our idea of necessity arises not simply from the events themselves but from our attitude towards them. The point is, however, that we *express* this attitude; we do not *state* it. Thus when we speak of events as causally related we convey as much about ourselves as about the events but we do so by speaking about the events not about ourselves.

In the above statement of his conclusion, the baleful effect of Hume's mechanical model is especially evident. Thus he has slipped back into treating an attitude as an object in the mind, mechanically arising there as a passive effect. In fact, an attitude is *intentional*. It takes an object. In short it is essentially directed towards the world. Thus if I feel certain about a process, I treat the *process* as certain. Precisely what I do not suppose is that there is no certainty in the process but only in myself. For then I should not be certain at all. In a sense, Hume acknowledges the point.

> Tis a common observation, that the mind has a great propensity to spread itself on external objects, and to conjoin with them any internal impressions, which they occasion, and which always make their appearance at the same time that these objects discover themselves to the senses.

The trouble is that he treats this tendency of the mind 'to spread itself on external objects' as though it were a form of popular illusion. In fact it should figure as an essential element in his account. For that tendency of the mind to spread itself on external objects is only its instinctive adaptation to the world. Thus our instinctive certainty that the effect will follow the cause is not a private event related only by accident to external occurrence. It is the way we adapt to the world. This adaptation occurs by instinct rather than reason because until we are adapted to the world we cannot reason about it at all. Thus nature does not *explain* wherein the certainty of causation lies; nevertheless it ensures that we trust in its certainty. That is because it is not necessary to our survival that we understand causation; what is necessary is that we trust it. In essence, that is Hume's point.

Hume's final conclusion, then, is that our idea of causality arises from the instinctive or natural workings of the mind, not from any rational insight into the objective process. Consequently, in elucidating our idea of causality we provide no ultimate or metaphysical explanation for the nature of causality itself. We proceed simply by elucidating those facts, in themselves familiar, which are found in our ordinary observation of objects and in our reactions to what we observe. This provides no solutions to the problems that the metaphysician raises. But it enables us to *understand* why we cannot solve those problems. In this way, it gives all the satisfaction that the metaphysician can provide whilst freeing us from his delusions.

Hume's final move is precisely to summarize those familiar facts on which our idea of causality depends. He does so by supplying two definitions of the causal relation. It will be important to consider what he says.

> There may be two definitions given of this relation, which are only different by their presenting a different view of the same object, and making us consider it either as a *philosophical* or as a *natural* relation; either as a comparison of two ideas or as an association between them. We may define a *cause* to be 'an object precedent and contiguous to another, and where all the objects resembling the former, are plac'd in the like relations of precedency and contiguity, that resemble the latter'. If this definition be esteemed defective, because drawn from objects foreign to the cause, we may substitute

41

this other definition in its place, viz. 'A *cause* is an object precedent and contiguous to another, and so united with it, that the idea of the one determines the mind to form the idea of the other, and the impression of the one to form a more lively idea of the other.'[12]

The reason why we need to consider these definitions is that the first is often used to support the view that Hume identifies causality with constant conjunction. Taken out of context, it may appear to do so. For Hume defines a cause as an object of the type that is constantly conjoined with another. Taken in its context, however, the definition evidently deals with causality as a *philosophical relation*. Now, as we have seen, Hume has already stated that a philosophical relation cannot give us an adequate idea of causation.

> Thus tho' causation be *a philosophical* relation, as implying contiguity, succession and constant conjunction, yet 'tis so far as it is a *natural* relation, and produces an union amongst our ideas, that we are able to reason upon it or draw any inference from it.[13]

The mere idea that two objects are constantly conjoined will never give us the idea of causality. In addition, there must be a natural tendency to associate the two, to infer the one from the other. That is why Hume immediately proceeds to a second definition which refers to that tendency. We may note that even this definition is very rough. Thus what Hume gives us is a description of the tendency. But it is evidently the *operation* of the tendency, not its description, which gives the idea of causality. Thus I do not *conclude* that the first object is the cause of the second *on the basis of* noting a tendency in my mind to infer the one from the other. *In so far* as I have a tendency to infer the one from the other, I *already* have a tendency to treat the first as a cause and the second as its effect.

On reflection, it will be obvious that Hume does not intend these definitions to be exhaustive. His aim is merely to summarize those familiar facts on which our idea of causality is based. Thus the first summarizes the facts about external events as they appear in ordinary observation; the second, the facts about how we react to what we observe.

Hume and Kant

In considering Hume's analysis of causality, it is inevitable that one should consider how it is related to Kant's. In his *Prolegomena*, Kant made the famous remark that it was Hume's analysis which awoke him from his dogmatic slumber.[14] It will be useful, if only briefly, to consider how the views of the two philosophers are related.

In his early philosophy, Kant was influenced by the views of Leibniz and Wolff. He later took their views as typical of speculative metaphysics, the attempt to present a complete system of the world based on pure reason. Now Hume showed, first, that causal inference is fundamental in all our reasonings about matters of fact and, second, that causal inference is not based on pure reason. Independently of experience, we cannot infer an effect from a cause. But experience alone is not sufficient to explain why a cause is necessarily followed by its effect. It was this which awoke Kant from his dogmatic slumber. Our knowledge of the world involves a necessary or a priori element which is not explicable in analytic or purely rational terms.

Kant took Hume to be an unmitigated sceptic whose aim in his analysis was purely destructive. He failed to detect Hume's appeal to nature or to natural belief. In short, he entirely failed to detect the positive side of Hume's philosophy. Nevertheless, he recognized that Hume had raised a fundamental problem. How can we know, prior to any discovery, that what we discover will always conform to the category of cause and effect? Kant's solution is that a world which did not conform to this category would not for us be an intelligible world. The world can be known by us only so far as it appears through such categories as that of causality. Consequently, causality is not something we discover *in* the world. Already it is presupposed, wherever in the world we seek to make a discovery.

Kant believed that in order to appreciate the above point, a radical shift was needed in philosophical thought. He compared it with the revolution brought about in astronomy by Copernicus. Philosophers are concerned to know the world. They do not first consider what enables them to know it. In consequence, they assume, however tacitly, that the capacity of the human mind is unlimited. Proper reflection will reveal, however, that the world can be known only so far as it appears through those forms or categories which are suitable to the human mind. These forms or categories are not ordinarily noticed precisely because they are always present in the mind. Because they are not noticed, they are readily assumed not to exist at all. It is therefore easy to assume that the capacity of the human mind is unlimited. But check the impulse to know the world and reflect, first, on what enables us to know it. In reflection, there will appear what ordinarily is taken for granted. It will then be obvious that the world is known only through certain forms or categories. Amongst these, is the category of causality.

A second feature, distinctive of Kant's philosophy, follows from this. Grant that the world is known only so far as it appears through those categories. It follows that what does not so appear *cannot* be known. Here we have Kant's famous distinction between the phenomenal and the noumenal. It is a subject of dispute amongst his commentators. Roughly, there are two interpretations. According to the first, there are two worlds, one of which, the phenomenal, is the object of our minds, the other of which, the noumenal or the real world, is entirely unknown to us. In short, we are acquainted only with appearances and do not know the real world at all. There is evidence for this interpretation in Kant's writings but I do not believe it was what he intended. His view was that there is one world which appears to us in categories suitable to our minds but which in its ultimate nature transcends those categories. It is phenomenal, so far as it appears in those categories; it is noumenal, so far as it transcends them. On this view, we know the real world, not appearances distinct from it. As Kant himself said, one cannot be acquainted with an appearance but only *with something that appears.* What appears is the real world. It appears, however, not in its ultimate nature but in forms suitable to our minds.

There follows a third feature, distinctive of Kant's philosophy. Speculative metaphysics is an attempt to grasp the world in its ultimate nature. In this attempt, metaphysicians employ the categories or concepts through which the world appears to us. They have no other categories or concepts to employ. But then they are assuming that the world in its ultimate nature may be understood through categories already familiar to us. Kant shows in some detail that this view leads to confusion. Thus an ordinary category, such as that of cause and effect, when employed for metaphysical purposes invariably leads to antinomy or contradiction. This may be explained on either of two assumptions. We may assume that those categories are inherently contradictory. But then they would be unintelligible even in their ordinary employment, which is absurd. The alternative is that those categories are intelligible only relative to the human perspective. The antimonies which arise in their metaphysical employment are then readily explained as resulting from their *misuse.* This point, once recognized, undermines the whole of speculative metaphysics.

Now in all the features sketched above, Kant was anticipated by Hume, and even more evidently by the Scottish naturalists. To illustrate the point, let us consider the features in turn. The resemblance between Kant's so-called Copernican revolution and Hume's science of man is already apparent. Hume's point is precisely that philosophers should curb their impulse to know the world and consider first what enables them to know it. Hume speaks, it is true, not of categories but of fundamental beliefs, ideas or principles. But what makes them fundamental? What are their chief characteristics? We find that they are not analytic. For example, one may deny without contradiction that an event has a cause. Nevertheless, they are inevitable features of the mind which are not themselves discovered but are presupposed in all our discoveries. In short, they are a priori faculties of the mind without which we cannot understand the world. Here we have many of the essential features of Kant's categories. The point is even more evident in Reid. Thus Reid speaks not of categories but of the principles of common sense. The usual mark of such a principle is that it may be denied without contradiction but not without absurdity. One of Reid's main points is that philosophers wander into absurdity because they suppose that anything may be disputed so long as it is free from contradiction. In that way, they lose contact with those fundamental principles, apparent in reflections, on which all genuine reasoning depends.

It will be equally apparent that Kant's distinction between the phenomenal and the noumenal is very similar to the one which Hume draws between the manifest and the ultimate. Here is an example from Hume, taken more or less at random.

> As long as we confine our speculations to *the appearances* of objects to our senses, without entering into disquisitions concerning their real nature and operations, we are safe from all difficulties, and can never be embarass'd by any question.[15]

Indeed, if my interpretation of Kant's distinction is correct, the two distinctions are virtually identical.

Hume and Kant differ in their approach to speculative metaphysics. Nevertheless the differences are less striking than the resemblances. Thus for both, there is as it were an excess of force in reason which drives it beyond the limits of its fruitful employment. Both find in this the source of speculative metaphysics and both find the cure for this disorder in a reflection on genuine reasoning which will reveal its limits.

We may turn now more specifically to the analysis of causality. The resemblances between the two philosophers are equally apparent. For both, our idea of causality is not derived from any insight into its ultimate base, for this is unknown. For both, the relation between cause and effect is not analytic; nevertheless it is a priori, for it is not simply the product of observation. For both, it is a *condition* rather than a *result* of our reasoning about matters of fact; and so on.

Nevertheless there is one important difference between the two philosophers. Hume's account is limited by his mechanical model of the relation between mind and the world. He is careful to emphasize that this model is not adequate to explain the ultimate nature of the relation. But it is plainly not adequate to deal even with those aspects of the relation which are apparent to us. In this respect there is an advance in Kant. For he conveys the idea that sense experience is rather an interpretation of the world than its mechanical effect. Consider, for example, the perception of a stationary object, such as a house. As Kant emphasizes, the sense experience which is involved in this perception cannot take the form of a static copy or picture. For it is in a continual process of change. Thus your sense experience changes as your eyes move from the lower part of the house through the middle to the top. How is a stationary or static object perceived through sense experience which is itself changing? A little reflection will reveal that the sense experience involved in perception is related to its object rather as a sign is related to what it signifies than as an effect is related to its cause. Thus the one may be related to the other *through a rule of translation*. Kant of course does *not* mean that the existence of an object is inferred in perception by reference to an explicit rule. He means that the relation may be represented in the form of a rule. In the case of perceiving the house, the rule is that of reversibility. Thus if you move your eyes from the floor to the roof and then from the roof back to the floor, your sense experiences repeat themselves in reverse order. This *means* that the object is static or stationary. In short, sense experience symbolizes rather than copies its object. Kant considers, also, how through changing sense experience one may perceive an object which is really changing. How is objective distinguished from subjective change? The mind's inherent grasp of causality plays an essential part in Kant's account. But the details of this account are not important for our purpose. What is important is that for Kant our grasp of causality involves relations to the world which are not mechanical but are intentional or purposive.

In this, Kant was not anticipated by Hume. Nevertheless, he was certainly anticipated by Reid. Thus Reid refers to sense experiences as *natural signs*. The sensation of touch will illustrate his point. It is evidently through sensations in the hand, or other parts of the body, that I am aware of the objects I touch. But what is the relation between the two? Do I infer the existence of the object from the existence of sensations in my hand, as I might infer a cause from its effect? In fact, when I touch an object, I am scarcely conscious of any sensations in my hand, being immediately aware of the object. In order to be aware of the sensations, I should need to repeat the process, this time concentrating on my hand. It is noticeable that when I do so I am no longer aware of the object. Plainly, therefore, in any ordinary sense, I do not infer the object from my sensations. Indeed the process is rather the reverse. So far from inferring the object from my sensations, I have to presuppose the object and infer what sensations I have when I touch it. Nevertheless, it seems evident that I should not be aware of the object unless I had sensation in my hand. Indeed, the point is easily proved, since when my hand is deprived of sensation or feeling, I am no longer aware of touching an object.

Here we have the problem which bedevils the philosophy of perception. Is perception direct or indirect, immediate or mediated? Each view is momentarily compelling; neither is ultimately satisfactory. Reid, it seems to me, was the first philosopher to solve this problem. Perception is both direct and indirect, immediate and mediated, depending on how one takes those terms. Thus it is immediate or direct, in the sense that it does not depend on inference, but it is mediated or indirect, in the sense that it presupposes processes distinct from the object perceived. This may still seem mysterious. But take a familiar instance of the process. When you read a book, you do not infer the meaning of the words from the letters on the page. You are scarcely conscious of the letters and are *immediately* aware of their meaning. It is obvious, however, that the meaning is *mediated* through those letters. The relation between sensation and its object is similar. When you concentrate on the letters, say in proof-reading, you lose their meaning. But when you cease to concentrate in that way, the meaning returns. Similarly, if you concentrate on the sensations in your hand, you lose awareness of their object. But this awareness returns when you cease to concentrate in that way. The sensations call attention not to themselves but to their object as the letters call attention not to themselves but to their meaning. Explicit signs, of course, are learned, unlike sensations. Reid's great insight, however, is that the processes involved in learning explicit signs presuppose others akin to those which are *not* learned. Explicit signs presuppose *natural* ones. Thus in sense experience the mind is related to the world not as a mechanical effect to its cause but as a sign to what it signifies.

Conclusion

Hume's analysis of causality is important, not simply in its own right but also for the light it throws on his philosophy more generally. To illustrate the point, it will be useful to contrast his view with those commonly found amongst other philosophers. On Hume's view, our idea of causality arises not from an insight into the objective process but from the instinctive or natural workings of the mind. Now many a philosopher would argue that this is unsatisfactory. Hume may be correct in *describing* how we arrive at the idea of causal necessity. What he has not shown is that this idea is *justified*. Thus our attitude to causality, though natural, might be mistaken; the process might not be as reliable as we take it to be. So far as it goes, this is perfectly true. But the question is: what follows from this? Many a philosopher would reply that we should set aside our natural attitude and examine the objective process. Only in this way can we tell whether we are justified in trusting it. Those who follow this procedure arrive at a number of different positions. We may consider first what might be termed metaphysical naturalism. On this view, there is nothing to causality but constant conjunction.[16] Constant conjunction may be determined by observation. Instinctive trust is therefore irrelevant. Observation is sufficient to confirm the certainty of the whole process.

We may note that such a philosopher seeks to determine the ultimate nature of causation and has begun by setting aside our natural attitude towards it. From Hume's point of view, his approach therefore is essentially metaphysical. Thus it is not based on ordinary reasoning for in ordinary reasoning our natural attitude is *not* set aside; indeed it is basic. From Hume's point of view, such a philosopher will therefore labour under two disadvantages. The first is that he cannot convince other philosophers that his view is true. He cannot establish, to the satisfaction of others, that there is nothing to causality but constant conjunction. The second is that his philosophical view is in conflict with his own natural attitude, as it is revealed in all his other dealings. For in all his other dealings, he places a trust in the causal process which would not be justified were there nothing to it but constant conjunction.

We may take, by contrast, the philosopher who seeks to show, on metaphysical ground, that there is *more to causation than constant conjunction*.[17] This view is consistent with his natural attitude. Unfortunately, he cannot persuade his opponents that it is true. Consequently he is in the same position as the vulgar, except that he is less clear than they, since he believes falsely that he can justify what they are content to take on trust.

There are philosophers, also, who agree that our natural attitude cannot be justified on metaphysical ground but who conclude that we are therefore not entitled to hold it.[18] This sceptical view presupposes that metaphysical reasoning carries more authority than our natural attitude itself. That is what Hume denies. Moreover, those philosophers in their normal dealings do put their trust in the causal process, which contradicts their philosophy.

Hume's view, in short, is that if we confine ourselves to our natural attitude, we may reason to some purpose. For example, we may persuade others and increase our knowledge. By contrast, if we set aside our natural attitude and attempt to support causal reasoning on a metaphysical base, we may certainly start many a dispute but we shall arrive at no solid conclusion.

Here we have the strain of epistemological naturalism which runs through Hume's philosophy. Our understanding of the world rests on knowledge which is grasped in practice but which cannot itself be justified in theoretical terms. It follows that we should eschew all speculation about ultimate causes. Since we cannot explain the basis of our knowledge, it is unlikely that we shall explain the nature of the whole universe. The analysis of causality serves both to illustrate and to support this view. Causal reasoning is a process entirely familiar to us; it enters at some point into all our dealings. Yet in theoretical terms, we do not understand causation at all. It is not likely that we shall understand the ultimate nature of the universe if we cannot understand a process so familiar. The moral is that we should eschew metaphysics and confine ourselves to common sense and empirical science, to those areas where we may hope to reason with some profit.

5

SCEPTICISM

Hume's philosophy in the *Treatise* draws a limit to knowledge or under-standing. This philosophy will therefore strike some as sceptical. In the final part of Book I, Hume considers how his views are related to the scepticism which has flourished in the history of philosophy. He argues in effect that his views constitute a form of mitigated scepticism and that this should be distin-guished from Pyrrhonism or total scepticism.[1] He argues, further, that total scepticism arises from an unbridled use of reason. There is in reason a tendency to become autonomous, to work out of relation to our other facul-ties and therefore to go beyond its natural limits. In this condition, it raises questions it cannot answer, becomes involved in contradictions, and reduces the mind to a universal doubt. Reason, in short, no less than the body, is liable to corruption. The cure is to cast a sceptical eye on reason itself. For this purpose, we need a mitigated scepticism which does not deny the use of reason but which understands its limits. A mitigated scepticism is therefore the cure for a total scepticism. In the course of his discussion, Hume considers our idea of the self and of the independent world. His treatment of these ideas is intended to be parallel to his treatment of causality. He seeks to show, for example, that our idea of an independent world is not produced by reasoning but by the workings of a natural tendency. As we have suggested, however, his treatment is altogether less successful, so that there are passages which run out of control and the author becomes involved in the scepticism from which he seeks to deliver us. It is these passages, as much as any, which support the idea that Hume is himself advancing a total scepticism. We shall return to this point. But first let us consider how Hume opens the final part of Book I.

He begins with an argument to illustrate how scepticism arises from an unbridled use of reason. The argument is compressed and some of its details obscure. Nevertheless, the principle behind it is clear enough. Having arrived at a judgement, I may reflect that my judgement in the past has not always been certain. This will cause me to reconsider my judgement. Suppose on checking this judgement, I find it confirmed. This will usually satisfy me. But if I am liable to error in my judgement, am I not thereby liable to error in judging that my original judgement is confirmed? In short, my doubt surely applies not simply to my original judgement but also to the process of checking it. Perhaps this process of checking should also be checked. But on reflection I realize that the doubt will apply also to this further process of checking, and so on ad infinitum, and at this point I realize also that I shall never remove it. I am reduced to scepticism. Once reason raises a doubt about itself, this doubt will apply to any reasoning that seeks to remove it. Consequently, reason can never remove a doubt about itself.

This argument is often said to be fallacious. It is said, for example, that my being mistaken in the past gives me no reason to suppose I am mistaken now. It does not follow that because I am mistaken on some occasions, I am always mistaken. It is true that this does not follow, but the objection entirely misses Hume's point. An analogy will make this clear. Suppose someone deceives you. It does not follow that he will always do so. Though untrustworthy in some areas, he may be trustworthy in others. That is true, but you will certainly not take *his* word for where he is or is not trustworthy. On that issue, the person has certainly lost his authority. Now your reason has deceived you. In other areas, it may be trustworthy. But, by a parallel argument, it is not your reason that can determine this. In short, it has lost all authority on where it is or is not trustworthy. But in that case you cannot trust it and are plunged once more into scepticism.

If we reflect on the above argument, however, we shall find that it does not lead as directly to scepticism as we have supposed. Strictly speaking, the argument simply shows that reason can raise a doubt which it cannot itself remove. To get to scepticism we need a further assumption. The assumption is that any doubt raised by reason must be removed by reason itself. In other words, if reason cannot remove a doubt nothing else legitimately can. Further reflection will reveal that this is equivalent to treating reason as an autonomous process to which all our other faculties are subordinate. Nothing else can remove a doubt it raises, for all else is subordinate to reason, which moves itself, independently of our other faculties and our relation to the world.

But let us consider for a moment how reason actually works. I recall my past errors and am depressed about my powers of judgement. I pass out of doors and note that the sun is shining. Not for a moment does it occur to me to doubt what I have just noted. A passer-by detains me, asking for directions to a certain place. I inform him. Turning towards my place of work, I quicken my pace because I think I may be late. I consider what task I shall first take up when I get there. Throughout the rest of the day I act and judge as I have always done. Here my doubts about my reason, or power of judgement, have been removed. But they have been removed through the situations in which I have found myself and through the revival of my faculties in general. In short, they have been removed not through the exercise of reason in itself but through its exercise in connection with my other faculties and my relation to the world. My reason has revived not through giving a direct answer to the question of whether it is trustworthy, but through answering other questions. As we have seen, however, it is no cause for scepticism that reason cannot give a direct answer to that question. Consequently, there is no cause for scepticism.

To see the point more clearly, let us consider again the steps of the sceptical argument. You can check a judgement; therefore you can check your checking; and you can check the checking of your checking. Here we have a recursive procedure which is certainly legitimate in itself. For example, such procedures are central in mathematics. Moreover, it is here being applied consistently. But what is its point? What function does it serve? Consider by contrast what occurs when I really check. I check because I am uneasy with my judgement. Perhaps this uneasiness arises from my reflecting that in this area I have sometimes gone astray But then this uneasiness has a function. It makes me return, with greater attention, to my material, the object of my judgement. For it is through my relation to this material, not through my own will, that my uneasiness arises. If I am still uneasy I check again. But suppose my uneasiness is removed. Then I have no freedom to doubt. I am not free since my doubt or uneasiness did not depend in the first place on my own will. It lay in my relation to my material and it is this relation which throughout controls my checking. Consequently, if my checking removes my uneasiness, there is no longer anything in the material that I find doubtful. Now return for a moment to the sceptical argument and you will find that it presents the merest parody of the checking process. Thus the process which sustains it is entirely internal. Lacking any relation to independent material, there is nothing to control it. It is not surprising that it should generate a doubt impossible to control.

Reasoning is a natural process. Like any other, it has its corruptions; but these occur when it is not performing its function. And this function, obviously enough, does not lie in its own workings but in its relation to something other than itself. Now these points are implicit in Hume's own views. In a famous passage, referring to the sceptical argument, he expresses them as follows.

> Shou'd it here be ask'd me, whether I sincerely assent to this argument, which I seem to take such pains to inculcate, and whether I be really one of those sceptics, who hold that all is uncertain, and that our judgment is not in *any* thing possest of *any* measure of truth and falsehood; I shou'd reply, that this question is entirely superfluous, and that neither I, nor any other person was ever sincerely and constantly of that opinion. Nature, by an absolute and uncontrollable necessity has determn'd us to judge, as well as to breathe and feel; nor can we any more forbear viewing certain objects in a stronger and fuller light, upon account of their customary connexion with a present impression, than we can hinder ourselves from thinking as long as we

are awake, or seeing the surrounding bodies, when we turn our eyes towards them in broad sunshine. Whoever has taken the pains to refute the cavils of this *total* scepticism, has really disputed without an antagonist, and endeavour'd by arguments to establish a faculty, which nature has antecedently implanted in the mind, and render'd unavoidable.[2]

The important point in this passage is usually taken to be that reasoning is as *unavoidable* as breathing or feeling. But an equally important point is that it is just as *natural*. It is evidently absurd to suppose that breathing sustains itself by its own motion, independently of its relation to the rest of the body and to the environment. But the same is true of reasoning. It can judge the world only because it is already related to the world in ways which are not of its own making.

In this respect, it is illuminating to compare Hume's view of reason with that of the Calvinists. Hume was no friend of Calvinism in its popular form. But, as we have already suggested, his view of reason is strikingly similar to that of the Calvinist theology. Thus the Calvinists advanced the doctrine of total corruption. This is not, as is vulgarly supposed, the view that human beings are totally evil. Rather, it is the view that human beings are liable to corruption in *all* their faculties. The view was advanced against those who criticized the doctrine of original sin, arguing that although human beings have a tendency to sin, they are free to restrain this tendency by the use of their reason and may therefore attain salvation by their own efforts. This view of reason, it may be noted, is similar to the one that Hume attacks throughout the *Treatise*. Roughly, it is the view that reason is an autonomous process to which all our other faculties are subordinate. Against this view, the Calvinists argued that human beings are as liable to corruption in their reason as in their other faculties. On the Calvinist view, our faculties are interrelated. You cannot separate a man's reasoning from the rest of him. Consequently, if you admit that there is corruption in any of his faculties, you thereby acknowledge that he is liable to corruption in them all. On this view, it is not through reasoning in itself that one arrives at the truth. One arrives at the truth by reasoning only if one is already *in* the truth. By this is meant related in the right way through all one's faculties to the world or to reality. Those not in that relation may reason correctly, in the sense that their reasoning is consistent or valid, but they will not arrive at the truth. Rather, by their reasoning they will be swept away from it.

It may be noted that Hume treats metaphysical reasoning in precisely that way. In other words, he treats it as a corruption of reason. Thus if we return for a moment to our sceptical argument, we find that it is not in itself inconsistent or invalid. Its fault is that its reasoning has become autonomous and has lost connection with the exercise of our other faculties and through them with the world.[3] Reasoning in this way is corrupt for its tendency is to undermine our natural beliefs and thereby to undermine reason itself. Later in this section, Hume expresses this view in an extreme form. He argues, as we shall see, that our natural beliefs lead inevitably on the level of metaphysical reasoning to antinomy or contradiction. The principle of causality, for example, has implications which if developed in an unrestrained way will undermine our belief in an independent world. His view, in short, is that the unrestrained exercise of reasoning inevitably undermines the beliefs on which reason depends and thereby undermines itself. This view, which is unintelligible on the enlightenment idea of reason, becomes immediately intelligible when one realizes that Hume's own idea is comparable with that of the Calvinists.

The idea of an independent world

Hume now turns to scepticism with regard to the senses. He will deal, in other words, with scepticism about an independent world. He begins by stating that the existence of such a world is not at issue.

> We may well ask, *What causes induce us to believe in the existence of body?* but 'tis in vain to ask, *Whether there be body or not?* That is a point, which we must take for granted in all our reasonings.[4]

What is at issue is not the truth of our belief in an independent world but how that belief arises. Hume's aim is to show that it arises not through sense experience or reason but through what he calls the imagination. In other words, it is the product rather of the mind's own workings than of what is supplied to the mind by sense experience or reasoning. In short, it is a priori. Hume's treatment, therefore, is parallel to his treatment of causality. He will show that our idea of an independent world is a natural belief on which reason and sense experience themselves depend.

Hume now says that our belief in an independent world involves two ideas which are intimately related but which may be separated for the purpose of analysis. The first is the idea of *continued*, the second that of *distinct* existence. Thus the existence of an independent world is *distinct* from our perceiving it and *continues* when we no longer do so. He proceeds to argue that these ideas cannot arise either through the senses or through reasoning. Let us begin with the senses.

It is immediately evident that the senses cannot give rise to the idea of *continued* existence, for the essence of such an existence is that it continues whether or not it appears to the senses. Sight alone, for example, obviously cannot establish that something exists when it is not seen. There remains the idea of *distinct* existence. Can this idea arise through the senses? Hume argues that this is impossible. His argument is as follows.

53

That our senses offer not their impressions as the images of some-thing *distinct*, or *independent*, and *external*, is evident; because they convey to us nothing but a single perception, and never give us the least intimation of any thing beyond. A single perception can never produce the idea of a double existence, but by some inference either of the reason or imagination. When the mind looks farther than what immediately appears to it, its conclusions can never be put to the account of the senses; and it certainly looks farther, when from a single perception it infers a double existence, and supposes the rela-tions of resemblance and causation betwixt them.[5]

Hume's argument is that in order to perceive an object distinct from ourselves, we should need to perceive *two* objects. Thus in order to perceive a tree, external to myself, I should need to perceive, first, its impression and, second, the tree itself. But this is impossible. The existence of the tree itself can only be an *inference*, because my perception can have only *one* object, namely, the *impression* of the tree. Now if by the impression of the tree, Hume means the sensory experiences involved in perceiving it, we may certainly allow that these are distinct from the tree itself. It is obvious, however, as Reid said, that Hume's argument will work only if we identify the object of my perception not with the tree but with those sense experiences. In effect, this is to say that the only thing I ever really see is my own seeing. It is obvious, in other words, that the whole argument rests on the fallacy noted by Reid. Hume has confused *what* I see with that *whereby* I see it. We may note that his use of the term 'impression' might have been calculated to bring this about, for it covers both the *object* of my perception and the *sensory experience* involved in perceiving it. The idea is then easily conveyed that the only object of perception is my own sense experience; in short, is mental or subjective. It now follows that an external object can never be the object of my perception. For an external object, by definition, is what is *not* mental or subjective. Having established this conclusion, Hume finds it easy to deal with objections to his view that the senses cannot give rise to the idea of distinct existence. For example, he considers the criticism that in perception we can distinguish between ourselves and objects distinct from ourselves. Thus I can distinguish the tree over there from myself, sitting here. Hume replies that, strictly speaking, what I see is not myself but *impressions* of my own body. These impressions are mental or subjective. Consequently, I do not see any distinct or external object.

Having established, to his own satisfaction, that the idea of an independent world cannot arise through the senses, Hume next considers whether it might arise through reasoning. He begins by pointing out that very young children readily engage with external objects. Consequently, the idea of an indepen-dent world is implicit in their actions, long before they might be led to it by any process of reasoning. This argument, it may be noted, does not depend on his empiricist assumptions. Those assumptions, however, very soon reappear. Hume argues that the way in which children, peasants, indeed the bulk of mankind, arrive at the idea of an independent world is not simply independent of reason but is in fact based on a delusion.

> For philosophy informs us, that every thing, which appears to the mind, is nothing but a perception, and is interrupted, and dependent on the mind; whereas the vulgar confound perceptions and objects, and attribute a distinct continued existence to the very things they feel or see. This sentiment, then, as it is entirely unreasonable, must proceed from some other faculty than the understanding.[6]

This argument plainly depends on his empiricist assumptions. The vulgar assume in perception that they are immediately aware of distinct objects. *But the only object of perception is a subjective impression.* Consequently, the vulgar must confuse subjective impressions with distinct objects. In short, they are under the delusion that what passes through their minds exists outside them. The difficulties in this view are very hard to exaggerate. Hume is asking us to accept that our very idea of independent objects arises from our confusing them with subjective impression. But it is hard to see how we can confuse the two unless we already have the idea of both. If we do not already have the idea of independent objects how can we confuse them with subjective impressions. Moreover, even if this can be explained, we are being asked further to accept that our very contact with reality depends on what in effect is a gross delusion. We shall return to these points.

Hume has established that our idea of an independent world does not in fact arise through reasoning. He argues further that if we turn to the reasoning offered by philosophers, we find that it cannot in any case give rise to the idea of an independent world. The philosophers are aware that the only objects of our perceptions are subjective impressions.[7] To this extent, they are better informed than the vulgar. They argue, however, that these subjective impressions can be explained as the effect of distinct objects. Consequently, we may arrive at the existence of independent objects by an inference from those subjective impressions. Hume's view is that this argument is contradictory. To establish the existence of external objects, the philosophers employ the principle of cause and effect. Thus our impressions are effects of external objects. It is noticeable, however, that they have experience only of the effects, the subjective impressions, and not of the causes, the external objects. But this is contradictory, for the principle of cause and effect requires that we have experience not simply of the effects but also of their causes. Having recognized that the only objects of perception are subjective impressions, the philosophers should have gone on, in terms of pure reason, to reject the idea of external objects. But their instinctive belief in an independent world is too strong for them. They therefore attempt incoherently to combine that view with the view that the only object of perceptions are subjective impressions. In consequence their view has all the difficulties of the vulgar together with others peculiar to itself.

Hume has now established, to his own satisfaction, that the idea of an independent world arises neither through reason nor through the senses. He will now proceed to give his own account of how it arises. We may note, once again, that his treatment is parallel to his treatment of causality. He takes an idea common to the vulgar, fundamental to our thinking. He shows that this idea cannot be justified by reference to any insight into the objective process. The attempt to do so results in a false philosophy. He will show that we are inevitably committed to this idea, which arises through the natural or instinctive workings of the mind. This is true philosophy.[8] The true philosophy differs from the false in that it holds the same views of the world as the vulgar. It differs from the vulgar in that it *understands* why we must rest content with those views.

But the parallel with causality ends at this point. For Hume's empiricist assumptions do not simply enter into his treatment of our idea of an independent world. Rather they form its basis. Thus he takes as fundamental that the only objects of our perception are subjective impressions. He must now show how we obtain the idea of a world external to them. But he has nothing to work with, except factors equally subjective. Thus association is a subjective mechanism which works with ideas as subjective as the impressions that give rise to them. As Reid said, the only consequence of these assumptions is a real scepticism. Moreover, Hume in some degree is aware of this. Hence the passages which run out of control, where he expresses the feeling that he has fallen into the scepticism he seeks to avoid. To see this more clearly, let us turn to his positive account.

As one might imagine, it is somewhat complicated. We shall take it in summary form. Here is Hume's own summary.

> The imagination naturally runs on in this train of thinking. Our perceptions are our only objects: Resembling perceptions are the same, however broken or interrupted in their appearance: This appearing interruption is contrary to the identity: The interruption consequently extends not beyond the appearance, and the perception or object really continues to exist, even when absent from us: our sensible perceptions have, therefore, a continu'd and uninterrupted existence.[9]

An example will illustrate what Hume means. Suppose I spend an hour or two gazing at a meadow. Then I retire for tea. Later I return to gazing at the meadow. Now on Hume's view what I see after tea is totally distinct from what I saw before. By this he means that the subjective impressions I receive are numerically distinct from those I received before tea. This is obvious since they are separated by the interval when I was away from the meadow. Nevertheless they are so exceedingly *like* those earlier impression that the mind is disposed to treat them as the same. That indeed is a natural tendency of the mind. A succession of elements qualitatively identical is naturally treated by the mind as a unity. Unfortunately there is a difficulty. The impressions cannot constitute a unity if they are separated by the interval when I was at tea. To cover this difficulty, the mind *feigns* that the impressions existed *during* that interval. In this way, out of elements subjective and different, the mind arrives at the idea of a continuously existing objective world.

Now Hume's account is supposed to describe the process which *gives rise* to our idea of an independent world. In fact, however, the idea of independent existence enters into that very process. Thus the mind treats different impressions as a unity. So far, the process is purely subjective. To preserve this unity the mind has to feign the independent existence of those impressions. But how does the mind get the sense of independent existence which is involved in feigning this? It is hard to see how the mind could feign the independent existence of subjective impressions unless it already has some idea of independent existence. But then it is unnecessary for it to feign the independent existence of subjective impressions.

To clarify the point, let us return to our example. In order to preserve the unity in my impressions of the meadow, I feign that they existed in the interval when I was away. But how do I conceive of their thus existing? Suppose I have an image of the meadow. What makes this more than another subjective impression? What gives it an objective reference? Hume here has the same difficulties as he had in explaining memory. On his account, I recollect a past event by having an image that copies or refers to it. But there is nothing in the image, when taken in itself, which gives it such a reference. Unless I already had some awareness of the past event, I could not know that my image copies or refers to it. Similarly, unless I have some sense of an independent or objective world, I cannot know that my subjective impressions have independent or objective reference. But, again, if I already have this sense, I do not need to obtain it by feigning the independent existence of subjective impressions.

It may be said, however, that we here overlook a point which we have emphasized earlier. Hume is not attempting to give an ultimate explanation of how we obtain the idea of an independent world. He wishes merely to describe some of the processes involved in our doing so. The answer to this is that the processes he describes are not really coherent. Moreover, they have not arisen through independent reflection but have been forced on him by his empiricist assumptions. Given those assumptions, for example, he cannot give any account of how the idea arises without attributing to the mind some form of gross delusion. In this respect, it will be useful to make a contrast with Kant. On Kant's view, fundamental ideas may be shown, by consistent reasoning, to involve antinomies or contradictions. Kant is careful to emphasize, however, that these arise not in the normal functioning of those ideas but only when they are treated as absolute. Moreover, he takes this as a proof that these ideas are *not* absolute in their function; they are valid only relative to the human perspective. In this way, he shows that these antinomies or contradictions are merely apparent. For Hume, by contrast, we are involved in contradiction or delusion even in the normal employment of our idea of an independent world. Moreover, this contradiction or delusion is not apparent but real. Thus we arrive at the idea of an independent world because we are under the delusion that our own sense experience exists outside us.

The difficulties do not lie in the conclusion which Hume seeks to establish. He is correct in supposing that our idea of an independent world is not the product of sense experience or reasoning. As he himself implies, young children readily engage with external objects. The idea of an independent world is therefore already implicit in their actions. Moreover, it is evident that in all our experience or reasoning we presuppose that we are related to an independent world. Hume's difficulties arise because his empiricist assumptions prevent his giving adequate expression to these views.

Conclusion

Before concluding Book I, Hume discusses our idea of the self. The issues he raises, so far as they are relevant to our purposes, have been covered in dealing with his treatment of our other fundamental ideas. Therefore we shall deal briefly with what he says.

His analysis is at its most powerful in its criticism of the idea that the self is a mental substance. He argues that he can detect no such persisting entity. The mind is a bundle of impressions. In support of this view, he examines identity more generally. He argues, for example, that the identity of a physical object lies not in a single persisting element but in the relations between various elements. Thus as the acorn develops into the oak, it changes continually both in form and matter. The unity lies in the relations that hold amongst the changing elements. The unity of the self is similarly to be explained.

Yet nowhere in his analysis does Hume treat the self as an embodied person having relations with other persons and with the world more generally. Indeed, he refers to the self as though it were nothing but a succession of impressions. Moreover, in dealing with identity in general, he often suggests that his analysis serves to undermine rather than to elucidate the ordinary notion. Thus he refers to it as a fiction and implies that in our ordinary dealings we are continually misled into supposing that there is a single persisting entity where none in fact exists. In short, his analysis of the self reveals that mixture of naturalism and empiricism which we have detected in his treatment of our other fundamental ideas.

Hume's account of our fundamental ideas is now complete. He has shown in each case that these ideas arise not as the product of our reasoning or experience but through the natural or instinctive workings of our minds. The conclusion should now follow naturally. Our fundamental ideas, being independent of reason, are impervious to it. Reason, since it depends on those ideas, cannot undermine them. Scepticism is easily avoided.

But having completed his analysis, he is no longer so sure. The trouble is that he has been unable to describe the natural or instinctive workings of the mind without attributing error or delusion to those very workings. On reflection, why trust them? The situation is made worse by the thought that our fundamental ideas exhibit conflict even amongst themselves. Thus in all our thoughts we rely on the principles of an independent world and of causality. As we have seen, however, Hume believes that the principle of causality has implications which will undermine that of an independent world. Thus in moving from subjective impressions to an external world we ought to rely on the principle of causality, for we have no other principle with which to determine any matter of fact. Yet, the principle forbids our moving from one to the other, for we have no experience of an external world but only of our subjective impressions. It is useless therefore to rely on reason in order to remove the conflicts and delusions involved in the workings of our minds. Reason serves only to reveal and to intensify those conflicts, so how can it remove them?

At the opening of the concluding section, we find therefore that Hume has succumbed to the very scepticism from which he promised to deliver us.

> My memory of past errors and perplexities, makes me diffident for the future. The wretched condition, weakness, and disorder of the faculties, I must employ in any enquiries, increase my apprehensions. And the impossibility of amending or correcting these faculties, reduces me almost to despair, and makes me resolve to perish on the barren rock, on which I am at present, rather than venture myself upon that boundless ocean, which runs into immensity. This sudden view of my danger strikes me with melancholy; and as 'tis usual for that passion, above all others, to indulge itself; I cannot forbear feeding my despair, with all those desponding reflections, which the present subject furnishes me with in such abundance.[10]

Now let us emphasize that this despair has its source in Hume's empiricism, not in his naturalism. His account of our idea of an independent world, so far as it is naturalistic, requires objective relations between the mind and the world. It cannot rest on subjective impressions. Unfortunately, on his empiricist assumptions, it is only in terms of subjective impressions that one can give an account of any idea. Consequently there is a conflict in his whole philosophy. We may note, also, that the incompatibility which he believes to hold between the principles of causality and of an independent world arises from the same source. Thus the incompatibility arises only if one assumes, first, that the only object of perception is one's own sense experience, and, second, that one can never move from one event to another unless one has repeatedly experienced instances of both. These assumptions, however, arise entirely from Hume's empiricism.

Book I is intended as a preliminary, giving the epistemological background to Hume's detailed study of human nature. The project threatens to end before the main study has begun. Nevertheless, what Hume describes in these pages is in the nature of a mood. He soon revives.

> Most fortunately it happens, that since reason is incapable of dispelling these clouds, nature herself suffices to that purpose, and cures me of this philosophical melancholy and delirium, either by relaxing this bent of mind, or by some avocation, and lively impression of my senses, which obliterates all these chimeras. I dine, I play a game of back-gammon, I converse, and am merry with my friends; and when after three or four hour's amusement, I wou'd return to these speculations, they appear so cold, and strain'd, and ridiculous, that I cannot find in my heart to enter them any further.[11]

Even this aversion to speculation soon passes. For with the revival of his faculties, there revives also his naturalism. 'Where reason is lively, and mixes itself with some propensity, it ought to be assented to.'[2]

Reason still has authority where it works in relation with those propensities which are fundamental in our lives and inevitably carry their force. Moreover, the impulse to know, to understand, is itself natural.

> I cannot forbear having a curiosity to be acquainted with the principles of moral good and evil, the nature and foundation of government, and the cause of those several passions and inclinations, which actuate and govern me. I am uneasy to think I approve of one object, and disapprove of another; call one thing beautiful, and another deformed; decide concerning truth and falsehood, reason and folly, without knowing upon what principles I proceed. I am concern'd for the condition of the learned world, which lies under such deplorable ignorance in all these particulars. I feel an ambition to arise in me of contributing to the instruction of mankind, and of acquiring a name by my inventions and discoveries. These sentiments spring up naturally in my present disposition; and shou'd I endeavour to banish them, by attaching myself to any other business or diversion, *I feel* I shou'd be a loser in point of pleasure; and this is the origin of my philosophy.[13]

Nature, reasserting its authority, will lead Hume into his detailed study of man. Nevertheless, he will retain elements of his scepticism. In particular, he will distrust the pretensions of reason, which has authority, he will recall, only when it depends on forces not themselves based on reason.

If we believe, that fire warms, or water refreshes, 'tis only because it costs us too much pains to think otherwise.[14]

6

THE PASSIONS

Book II of the *Treatise* is devoted to what would now be termed the philosophy of psychology. Hume analyses some of the most fundamental human passions and emotions. In its main drift, this is the least controversial section of the *Treatise*, for with regard to the passions, naturalism is inherently plausible. Few people would argue, for example, that sexual desire is acquired through reasoning or is the product of experience. Whatever the effect of experience or reasoning, it only too evidently has a base which is independent of both. Consequently we shall not follow Hume in detail but shall give an example of his procedure and then concentrate on the two most important sections in Book II, these being the discussions of free will and of the relation between reason and the passions.[1]

As an example of his procedure we may take his analysis of pride. At first sight, pride is occasioned by an enormous variety of objects. People may take pride in their children, in their home, in their art collection, and so on. At this level, pride may seem the product of social circumstances. Thus people can hardly take pride in their children if they live in a society, such as modern China, which seeks to restrict the size of the family, in their art collection, if they live in a society which places no value on art, or in their home, if they live among people who lead a nomadic existence. Hume shows that in all such cases we find a natural instinct working its way according to principles themselves natural, in the sense that they are independent of social circumstances. Thus it may be an accident of social circumstances that art collections are highly valued. But it is not such an accident that a proud man or woman in that society, other things being equal, will have a motive to acquire such a collection. For that is the natural working of pride.

In support of this view, Hume distinguishes between the *cause* and the *object* of pride, between the idea which excites the passion and that to which it is directed when excited. Thus it is the thought of the art collection which excites a person's pride but the object of that pride is in the thought that it is *his*. What is constant and original in the passion is that it has the self as its object. What is variable are the particular causes which excite it. To make this clear, Hume distinguishes in the cause between the subject, the art collection itself, and some quality it has, such as its beauty or its being valued by others. Whether the subject is an exciting cause will depend on its having such a quality and that will depend on varying circumstances. But that quality, in its turn, will give rise to pride only if it is associated with the self. Thus the thought that their collection is valued will give people pleasure but it is because the valued collection is theirs that their pleasure turns into pride. Thus behind the variations in exciting causes, we find an impulse which belongs to our nature. The passion runs constant; what varies are the opportunities for satisfying it.

Hume now translates this into his vocabulary of association, impression and idea. There is association between both ideas and impressions. The idea of dark clouds gives rise to the idea of rain. The impression or sensation of grief or disappointment gives rise to the impression of anger or envy. Now pride is characterized, says Hume, by a double association of ideas and impressions. If my art collection is valued, this idea will give rise to the idea that what is valued is *my* collection; the pleasure at its being valued will turn into the pleasure at its being *mine*; in short, it will turn into pride. In this process, we may substitute, in place of the valued art collection, an infinite number of other examples. Nevertheless, the process remains the same. In this way we easily introduce order into the bewildering variety of forms which pride appears to assume. Behind the variety, we find a natural passion working its way according to principles equally natural.

It will be noted that Hume, in the above analysis, avoids the fallacy of supposing that in explaining a human passion we have to choose between nature and nurture. He shows that the expression of pride, which varies according to nurture or social circumstances, requires a natural base and that the natural base, the passion itself, requires social circumstances or nature for its expression. Nature and nurture therefore are not opposed but are interrelated. Thus it is not part of our nature to take pride in an art collection. But pride is part of our nature and if we can be satisfied by an art collection we shall naturally take pride in it. Roughly speaking, nature gives us the general passion; how we satisfy it in particular circumstances depends on us.

The strength of Hume's account lies in its naturalistic base. The weakness, as usual, lies in its empiricism. Thus the idea that pride can be explained by the internal mechanism of association is quite spurious. To see this, let us consider for a moment what we mean by pride. Evidently, it cannot be defined purely as an inner impression or sensation which happens invariably to take the self as an object. The thought of self is integral to the passion. That indeed is why pride takes an object. It is intimately related to thought, which is intentional not mechanical. By contrast, a pure *sensation* never takes an object. A sensation of pain, for example, is not *about* anything.[2] An *emotion*, such as pride, takes an object but that is because it cannot be reduced to a mere sensation. It is a major weakness in Hume's account, throughout Books II and III, that his empiricism never allows him to distinguish clearly between sensation and emotion. Thus in pride, the sensation a person feels is no more important than the way he *thinks* and *acts*. Indeed, pride seems evidently to involve a level of thought which requires the concepts of a language. The passion, for example, is hardly discernible amongst the animals, or is discernible only in the most rudimentary form. That is because the passion requires not simply that one *is* a self or subject, but that one has the *concept* of oneself, in terms of which one can consciously distinguish oneself from others, and *dwell* in *thought* on the differences involved. This shows also that the difference between reason and passion is not as sharp as Hume usually supposes. By this we do not mean that a passion such as pride is *based* on reason or can be explained *purely* in terms of it. On that point, Hume is entirely correct. Nevertheless, the two are more closely related than he explicitly allows. We shall return to this point when we consider his account of the relation between reason and passion.

The will

Hume's section on the will almost immediately takes up the disputed question concerning *liberty* and *necessity*. He will deal, in short, with the issue of free will. On this issue, it is traditional to distinguish between two opposing positions. We have, on the one hand, the determinists and, on the other, the libertarians. The determinist argues that human action, no less than inert matter, is always determined or necessary and therefore cannot really be free. The libertarian argues that every genuine action is really free and therefore cannot be determined or necessary. Hume's discussion has been very influential, because he was amongst the first to adopt a position, sometimes called compatibilism, which is different from both the traditional ones.

Hume begins by considering what is meant by *necessity*. Here he relies on his analysis of causation. We know nothing of necessity as an objective quality. We treat a succession as necessary, not because we perceive necessity in its workings, but because it exhibits a certain degree of order or regularity. It exhibits the required degree when on the appearance of one of its elements we confidently infer the other. The question of whether human action is necessary reduces itself therefore to whether human action exhibits the required degree of order or regularity. To this, the libertarian would reply that the required degree occurs only in physical nature. Human action, unlike the operations of matter, cannot be predicted. The determinist, by contrast, would affirm that the required degree occurs alike in physical and in human nature. On this issue, Hume sides unequivocally with the determinist.

> Whether we consider mankind according to the difference of sexes, ages, governments, conditions, or methods of education; the same uniformity and regular operation of natural principles are discernible.

Like causes still produce like effects; in the same manner as in the mutual action of the elements and powers of nature.[3]

Hume recognizes that this is not immediately apparent.

Now some may, perhaps, find a pretext to deny this regular union and connexion. For what is more capricious than human actions? What is more inconstant than the desires of man? And what creature departs more widely, not only from right reason, but from his own character and disposition? An hour, a moment, is sufficient to make him change from one extreme to another, and overturn what cost the greatest pain and labour to establish. Necessity is regular and certain. Human conduct is irregular and uncertain. The one, therefore, proceeds not from the other.[4]

Hume argues, however, that the same point might have been made about physical nature. There, too, order or regularity is not *immediately* apparent. If you think differently, that is because you are influenced by the conclusions of science. But a scientist works in the closed environment of a laboratory. Outside the laboratory, order and regularity are immediately apparent only in the movements of the planets. Consider nature more generally and what is immediately apparent is inconstancy or change. Indeed the very symbol for inconstancy is found not in human action but in the wind, which blows where it listeth. For the most part, we believe in the order or regularity of nature because we believe it can be found there, not because it is immediately apparent. But why then should it be different in human affairs? Indeed if we reflect, we find that order or regularity is the very condition of social life. For example, it cannot be exceptional that people keep engagements. If it were exceptional, they would not be made in the first place. We predict behaviour not only in physical nature but also in human affairs and it is often more certain in human affairs than in physical nature. Hume gives an example.

A prisoner, who has neither money nor influence, discovers the impossibility of his escape, as well from the obstinacy of the gaoler, as from the walls and bars with which he is surrounded; and in all attempts for his freedom chooses rather to work upon the stone and iron of the one, than upon the inflexible nature of the other.[5]

The prisoner is less certain that he will be prevented in his escape by the walls than by the gaoler. He has a chance with the walls but he can predict with certainty that with the gaoler he has no chance at all. Moreover, prediction seems as compatible with action in the moral sphere as with action in any other. Suppose a person has to choose between good and evil. The better he is, the more certain one can be that he will choose the good. Consequently goodness seems to be compatible with predictability. Indeed the better the person, the easier he is to predict.

So far, then, Hume's account favours determinism. Nevertheless he is not concerned to deny free choice. That, indeed, is why his view is often termed compatibilism. To appreciate his view, we need to distinguish between what he calls liberty of spontaneity and liberty of indifference. It is only the latter he denies. Liberty of indifference means indifference to causal influence. The will is indifferent in the sense that it is independent. The explanation for an act lies in the will's own movement as distinct from some cause which brings it about. Liberty of spontaneity, by contrast, implies only that the will is independent of constraint. Now free choice, in the ordinary sense, implies spontaneity not indifference. Thus, in the ordinary sense, a man is unfree when he is forced to perform an act, whether or not he wishes to. He is free when he does what he wishes. The man who is free is not independent of all causes but only of those which operate from the outside and constrain him. So long as he does what he wishes, it is irrelevant whether his wishes themselves have their causes. For those causes work through his own mind, belong to him, and therefore cannot act as a constraint on what he wishes. Thus he is free as spontaneous, independent of constraint, not as indifferent, independent of all causes.

Hume's implication is that the problem of free will arises through a confusion between the different types of liberty. The libertarian, seeing that free choice is real, assumes liberty of indifference. The determinist, seeing that there is no liberty of indifference, assumes there is no free choice. In fact, both views rest on a common fallacy. They assume free choice requires liberty of indifference, when it requires only liberty of spontaneity.

Hume now argues that the kind of necessity which he attributes to human action, so far from subverting religion and morality, is in fact essential to both. For example, both in religion and in morality, a central place is given to reward and punishment. But we administer reward and punishment because we know that they operate on the human will as causes having regular effects. Through reward we shall promote virtue; through punishment we shall discourage vice. Neither could operate if the libertarian view were correct and the human will were indifferent to causes. Indeed we may go further. The libertarian view seems to divorce human action from that connection with its surroundings which is essential to its intelligibility. An example will illustrate the point. Suppose you are a passenger in a car, an obstacle looms, the driver applies the breaks. This might serve as the paradigm of a responsible action. Seeing the danger to the car and the harm to its passengers, the driver as a responsible individual has no alternative but to act as he does. Note however that the act is responsible, indeed intelligible, only in relation to its circumstances. *In the circumstances*, it was the *only* thing a responsible driver could do. Now suppose the driver tells you that he is a free individual and, as a matter of fact, in precisely these circumstances he might very well have chosen to do the exact opposite, allowing the two of you to crash into the obstacle. It is no longer possible to see his act as responsible; indeed it is hard to see it as an intelligible human act.

As we have said, Hume's account of liberty and necessity has been influential. It has been influential, for example, amongst scientific positivists who have used it to advocate the unity of science. They take Hume to have shown that causality is the same in human and physical nature. From this they infer that there is no difference in kind between the two. Human action differs only in degree from the behaviour of physical objects. This interpretation is based on the assumption that Hume identifies causality in its objective nature with regularity or constant conjunction. It is then assumed that causality must be identical in nature both in physical and human affairs, since regularity or constant conjunction is found in both.

Now it is important to see that this interpretation is mistaken. Hume is certainly not saying that causality is one in its nature and is identical with what we find in the physical world. Indeed this makes nonsense of his account. So far as a person's behaviour can be explained purely by physical causes, he is *not* free. In short, Hume's so-called compatibilism presupposes that the causation involved in human action is different from purely physical causation. The point will be evident if we return for a moment to our example of the car driver. As we have said, he has no alternative as a responsible individual but to act as he does. He cannot be responsible, however, unless he appreciates the situation in which he is placed. Now a piece of metal when placed in acid has no alternative but to dissolve. That, however, is not because it appreciates the situation in which it is placed. It is evident that causation in human action works through the agent's own understanding or belief. In other words, it involves concepts that have no application in the purely physical world. It is true that when Hume is in the grip of his empiricist assumptions, he insufficiently appreciates this point. But he appreciates it readily enough in the present context.

> Let no one, therefore, put an invidious construction on my words, by saying simply, that I assert the necessity of human actions, and place them on the same footing with the operations of senseless matter. I do not ascribe to the will that unintelligible necessity, which is suppos'd to lie in matter. But I ascribe to matter, that intelligible quality, call it necessity or not, which the most rigorous orthodoxy does or must allow to belong to the will. I change, therefore, nothing in the receiv'd systems with regard to the will, but only with regard to material objects.[6]

To understand the above passage, it is essential to realize that Hume is not claiming to reveal the true or ultimate nature of causality or necessity. A fortiori he is not claiming that it lies in regularity or constant conjunction. He states repeatedly that its true or ultimate nature is entirely unknown. All we know is that there is order or regularity both in human and in physical affairs. The ultimate nature of this order or regularity he does not pretend to explain. It is as mysterious in physical as in human affairs. Order or regularity, in both realms, is the reflection of deeper causes, themselves unknown. Consequently when he attributes necessity or causality to human actions, he simply means that in the human as in the physical realm there is order or regularity. That is the intelligible quality to which he refers in the above passage. As he says, he is not attributing to human actions that mysterious necessity, to him unintelligible, which philosophers claim to find in matter. He is merely attributing to human actions that order or regularity which anyone who reflects will readily allow.

> The only particular in which any one can differ from me, is either, that perhaps he will refuse to call this necessity. But as long as the meaning is understood, I hope the word can do no harm.[7]

The difference between Hume and such a person can only be verbal, for he does not attribute any quality to human actions which is not already known and acknowledged. Moreover, in claiming that there is order alike in the physical and in the human realm, he in no way implies that this order must take the same *form* in the two cases. That is why he rejects the claim that he is placing human actions on the same footing as senseless matter. There is order in both realms, but in the human realm it manifestly assumes forms altogether different from those found in the physical.

Reason and passion

Hume begins his account of the relation between reason and passion with a famous passage.

> Nothing is more usual in philosophy, and even in common life, than to talk of the combat of passion and reason, to give the preference to reason, and to assert that men are only so far virtuous as they conform themselves to its dictates. Every rational creature, 'tis said, is oblig'd to regulate his actions by reason; and if any other motive or principle challenge the direction of his conduct, he ought to oppose it, 'till it be entirely subdu'd, or at least brought to a conformity with that superior principle. On this method of thinking the greatest part of moral philosophy, ancient and modern, seems to be founded; nor is there an ampler field, as well for metaphysical arguments, as popular declarations, than this suppos'd preeminence of reason above passion. The eternity, invariableness, the divine origin of the former have been display'd to the best advantage: The blindness, unconstancy,

and deceitfulness of the latter have been as strongly insisted on. In order to show the fallacy of all this philosophy, I shall endeavour to prove *first*, that reason alone can never be a motive to any action of the will; and *secondly*, that it can never oppose passion in the direction of the will.[8]

As we have seen, Kemp Smith holds that the whole of Hume's philosophy is implicit in the above passage. Hume will reverse the classical view of human nature. We are moved by forces to which reason may contribute but which cannot be derived from reasoning. Man, therefore, is not, in the classical sense, a rational animal. Our reason assists the workings of our passions but as servant rather than as master. Properly, it is a subordinate faculty.

To establish this view, Hume distinguishes between two types of reasoning, the demonstrative and the probable. Demonstrative reasoning is found most commonly in logic and mathematics. In a syllogism, for example, the conclusion follows of necessity from the premise. If all Greeks are wise and Socrates is a Greek then necessarily Socrates is wise. Still, you do not know whether Socrates is wise. For that follows only if the premises are true. And to find whether the premises are true you have to consult the world. For that reason, Hume thinks it obvious that demonstrative reasoning in itself cannot move the will. For though it provides validity, it cannot provide any concrete matter of fact. It cannot provide anything concrete by which the will can be directed.

To provide that, you need to turn to probable reasoning. The term probable is technical. In ordinary speech, a conclusion is probable when it lacks complete certainty. In Hume's usage the term carries no such connotation. It just means non-demonstrative, and refers to the reasoning by which we infer effects from causes and determine matters of fact. At first sight, this type of reasoning does direct the will. For example, if you want to go to London and are informed that it is the road to the left rather than to the right, which leads there, you will take the one to the left. On reflection, however, it is obviously not the information in itself which directs your will. For if you had wanted not to go to London exactly the same information would have led you to the other road. How you are directed depends, primarily, on the end you pursue, which depends, in turn, on what you want. Reason, in short, is relevant to the means not the end; it determines not what you want but how to get it. Now the means, by definition, is subordinate to the end and therefore reason is subordinate to passion. For it is passion which determines the end and reason only the means.

Hume's first conclusion, then, is that reason alone can never be a motive to any action of the will. The second conclusion immediately follows. Reason alone can never oppose passion in directing the will. For since it can direct the will only through a passion, it can oppose one passion only through another. Strictly speaking, therefore, the conflict between reason and passion never occurs. There can be conflict only between different passions, each of which may or may not be assisted by reason. Hume summarizes his view in the famous statement: 'Reason is, and ought only to be the slave of the passions, and can never pretend to any other office than to serve and obey them.'[9]

Acknowledging that this view is controversial, Hume proceeds to elaborate it. He argues that a passion, when taken in itself, never represents the world. By this he means that in itself it involves no element of belief. Consequently it is neither true nor false; it just is. But then in itself it can never be in conflict either with truth or with reason.

> When I am angry, I am actually possest with the passion, and in that emotion have no more reference to any other object, than when I am thirsty, or sick, or more than five foot high. 'Tis impossible, there-fore, that this passion can be oppos'd by, or be contradictory to truth and reason; since this contradiction consists in the disagreement of ideas, consider'd as copies, with those objects, which they represent.

At this point, one may suspect that something has gone wrong with Hume's account. For he is now at the opposite extreme from the position he is attacking. Thus if my passion is a fact about me just like my being over five foot in height, one can easily appreciate that it cannot come into conflict with reason. But the difficulty now is to see how there can be any relation at all between the two. My height is a physical fact which is quite independent of what I think, whether about my height or about anything else. But surely there is some relation between thought and passion. For example, in ordinary speech it is perfectly intelligible to call a person's anger justified or unreason-able. No one can be called unreasonable for being more than five foot in height.

Hume is aware of this point and hastens to accommodate it to his account. He argues that a passion may be called unreasonable in either of two ways. The first is where a person is mistaken about the object of his passion. Suppose, for example, I am angry because I think you have insulted me. My anger may be called unreasonable if I have no good reason to think this. The second is where a person is mistaken in the means he adopts to satisfy a passion. I want to go to London but make a muddle of how to get there. What Hume argues, however, is that in both these types of case, it is not the passion which is unreasonable but rather the belief or judgement that accom-panies it. Strictly speaking, for example, what is unreasonable is not my anger but my belief that you have insulted me. 'In short, a passion must be accompa-ny'd with some false judgement, in order to its being unreasonable; and even then 'tis not the passion, properly speaking, which is unreasonable but the judgement.'[10]

We may feel that this does not altogether remove our difficulty. Thus to say that belief or judgement *accompanies* a passion is to suggest that the two are connected only accidentally. In fact my anger is hardly *intelligible* on this occasion unless I have some belief such as that you have insulted me. Indeed so close is the relation between the two, that when I become convinced that you have not insulted me, I cease to be angry with you. There is nothing in Hume's account to explain so intimate a relation between thought and passion. Moreover, so far from providing such an explanation, he continues to assert a position at the opposite extreme from the one he is attacking.

> Where a passion is neither founded on false suppositions, nor adopts means insufficient for the end, the understanding can neither justify nor condemn it. 'Tis not contrary to reason for me to prefer the destruction of the whole world to the scratching of my finger. 'Tis not contrary to reason for me to prefer my total ruin, to prevent the least uneasiness of an *Indian* or person wholly unknown to me. 'Tis as little contrary to reason to prefer even my own acknowledge'd lesser good to my greater, and have a more ardent affection for the former than the latter.[11]

This surely is still unsatisfactory. We may grant, in a sense, that the attitudes Hume mentions are not unreasonable. But that is because they are not sufficiently intelligible to be assessed in such terms. One can understand the over-sensitive person who continually suspects an insult, however unreasonable his attitude. But how is one to assess, in any terms, the attitude of a person who prefers his own destruction and that of the whole world rather than suffer a minor scratch to his finger? Without further background, one cannot understand what arouses him, how his mind works.

We shall return to the above points; but first we must complete our exposition of Hume's views in this section. He next distinguishes between calm and violent passion. We are often moved without violent feeling. Hume mentions as examples the instinct for preservation, kindness towards children, an appetite for the good. By contrast, other passions are violent. He mentions anger, resentment and grief.

Now Hume is here attempting to overcome a weakness which results from his inability to distinguish clearly between sensation and emotion. He is unable to do so, because on his official view every feeling is identified with some inner impression or sensation. But no emotion can be identified with an occurrent sensation or feeling. The point is evident in the case of anger. We associate anger with violence because of the way an angry person so often behaves, not because of the sensations he feels, of which in any case we are largely ignorant. As we have said, in distinguishing an emotion, what is important is the way a person is disposed to think and act. And it is evident that the way a person is disposed to think and act cannot be identified with any sensation he feels. Suppose, for example, that a person resolves to give up chocolate. A few days later he is gravely tempted. What he *feels* is desire for the chocolate. He may be so disposed that he overcomes this desire. But that disposition may be associated with no particular feeling at all. Again, it is an occasional drinker rather than the drunkard who is likely the more keenly to anticipate an evening's drinking. Nevertheless, it is the drunkard who is the more firmly disposed.

Now Hume's inability to distinguish disposition or emotion from occurrent feeling leads him into serious difficulties. Consider again the person who overcomes his desire for chocolate. On Hume's view, one passion can be overcome only by another. Consequently it is only through some other passion that this person can overcome his passion for chocolate. The difficulty is that if you identify passion with occurrent feeling, you cannot find the other passion. In terms of occurrent feeling, the only passion he feels is a desire for the chocolate. It is to avoid this difficulty that Hume distinguishes between calm and violent passion. He argues that what is identified with reason is still passion but passion in its calm rather than in its violent aspect. The terms are inadequate. But the point they inadequately express is sound in itself. To appreciate the point, we have only to consider our other example. By a parallel argument, it is reason which moves the drunkard. For he is not moved by occurrent feeling. Indeed it often happens that what the drunkard most keenly feels is the misery of his condition. Nevertheless he goes on drinking. It seems obvious that this is best explained through the working, not of his reason, but of an ingrained habit or disposition.

In assessing Hume's account of the relation between reason and passion, we must distinguish between his basic point and the way he develops it. In his basic point he expresses his naturalism. Reason alone cannot move the will. In other words, the forces which move us are given us by nature and are not the product of our reasoning. The difficulties in his account arise from the way he develops this point, and those difficulties, in turn, arise from assumptions which conflict with his naturalism. His naturalism demands that he consider the various faculties in relation to the whole person and the person in his relation to the world. But his empiricism hampers his doing so by forcing on him a subjective view of the mind. The effect is to separate the workings of a person's mind from his general engagement with the world.

To illustrate this point, let us consider how, on the naturalist view, we are to distinguish between sensation, emotion and reason. As we have emphasized, there is already a clear distinction between sensation and emotion, between, on the one hand, sensations of pain, hot and cold, itching, tickling, sinking in the stomach, and on the other emotions of anger, grief, love, jealousy. Thus a sensation takes no object. A sensation of pain, for example, is not *about* anything; it arises independently of thought and cannot be altered by any change in one's thinking. An emotion such as anger, by contrast, is intimately related to its object and as one changes in one's view of the object so one's anger intensifies or disappears. As we have said, Hume has no explanation for these differences. But they are readily intelligible once one takes them in relation to the teleology of the whole person. Thus a sensation of pain arouses our attention to some harm in the body, of which we should otherwise be unaware. Anger is a response to what is hostile in the environment. In a world which is often hostile or harmful, both have an obvious function in preserving the life of the whole organism. But they serve this function in different ways. Anger is intimately related to thought or attention, because without attending to the environment one cannot respond to it. It is essentially directed outwards, to an independent world. Pain, by contrast, cannot depend on attention, for its purpose is to arouse it and the attention once aroused is focused on ourselves. It is therefore obvious why, in identifying all feelings with sensations, such as pain, one separates the workings of the mind from its relation to an independent world.

A further point also becomes obvious. Anger *requires* thought or attention. The two do not simply accompany one another. Here we touch on the major defect in Hume's account. On the classical view, passion is subordinate to reason. Hume simply reverses the view. Reason is subordinate to passion. But if we attend to the teleology of our faculties, we find that although both passion and reason are subordinate to the workings of the whole organism, neither is subordinate to the other. Indeed their function in relation to the whole organism requires that they work together. Passion can no more work without reason than reason without passion. Thus there can be no response to what is hostile without a passion such as anger, but there can be no passion such as anger without thought or attention to what is hostile. Each requires the other.

We may elaborate the point by considering Hume's analysis of the relation between means and end. On his analysis, the end is given through passion; the means is determined through reason. As the means is subordinate to the end, so reason is subordinate to passion. But this is plausible only if one takes the means–end relation in abstraction from a person's life more generally. In the process of working out the means to an end, the end is given in the sense that one is wholly concerned, not with the end, but with how to achieve it. In that moment, one evaluates the means in the light of the end. But it is only for that moment. For having completed the process, one might then re-evaluate the end in the light of the means available. For example, suppose I work out that in order to get to London, I must travel in such and such a way at such and such a cost. I might then ask myself whether at such a cost I really want to go to London. Here it is the end which is being evaluated in the light of the means.

A little reflection will reveal that Hume's account cannot be correct. The means cannot simply be subordinate to the end, nor yet reason to passion. For the *character* of the end may change when I have appreciated the means available, the *character* of my desire when I have worked out what it involves. Thus my going to London is desirable before I have worked out how to get there. Afterwards it becomes a waste of my resources and ceases to be desirable.

The point can be developed by considering that our desires are various and that they are often in conflict. The means for satisfying one may prevent our satisfying another. Consequently we must reason as much about ends as means. Without some integration of our desires, we do not know which to satisfy and then it is idle to reason about means. Thus it is idle for me to work out how to get to London if I cannot work out how important it is for me to get there. In the process of integrating our desires, reason is indispensable. Moreover, the process could hardly occur unless passion were adjusted to reason.

We may give a further illustration of this point. The development of character demands the control of impulse. To be the victim of every impulse is to lack any definite character. One controls impulses by inhibiting one in favour of another. For example, one controls a present desire in order to obtain a greater good in the future. This requires, first, that ends be evaluated. One evaluates the future good as greater than the present one. This is impossible without reasoning. But it requires, second, that the teleology of the passions be adjusted to reason, or be implicitly rational, for otherwise it would be impossible, as a result of reasoning, to inhibit the present desire in favour of the future one. This of course does not mean that passion is controlled by reason *alone*. If that were true, at least in its extreme form, reason would never be ineffective, which is very far from being the case. Although reasoning is indispensable to evaluation, it always presupposes a sense of value which cannot arise through reasoning but only through natural desire. On that point, Hume is perfectly correct. Indeed it is evident that reason would be impotent to control desire unless in the teleology of the passions there were already a basic drive towards integration. The point is, however, that the drive itself requires reasoning and in some measure is adjusted to it. In short, we see once again that reason and passion are *interrelated*.

It will be useful, at this point, to return for a moment to Hume's claim that it is not unreasonable to prefer one's own destruction and that of the whole world rather than have one's finger scratched. As we said, there is a contrast between this case and that of the over-sensitive person who is forever suspecting an insult. The latter we find unreasonable but not unintelligible. It is now easy to see why this is so. Suspicion has an evident place within the teleology of the emotions. It is a feature of that alertness to what is hostile which helps to preserve our own interest. Consequently we readily understand the over-sensitive person. He exhibits in an extreme or distorted form an attitude which in itself has an obvious teleology. But it is hard to imagine how the attitude of the other person fits into any form of teleology. He *prefers* the destruction of the world to getting his finger scratched. But preference implies choice and therefore some form of comparison or assessment. The difficulty in this case is to imagine what form the assessment might take. According to what form of assessment is a scratch on the finger *worse* than the destruction of the world? To make the case at all intelligible we have to suppose an extreme disintegration of personality, having its source in some obscure form of causation. In short, we cannot treat him as a person but can only study him as an object whose behaviour is governed by causes rather than reasons. As we said, it is true in a sense that his attitude is not unreasonable but that is because he does not fall into the category of the reasonable. He cannot be assessed in those terms at all.

The same point applies to Hume's other examples in the passage we quoted. He claims, for example, that it is not unreasonable for a person to prefer his lesser to his greater good. But it is only through reasoning that the person can distinguish between the two in the first place. It is true that this reasoning may be ineffective. He may simply indulge his present impulse. It is intelligible enough in a given case. But if we suppose his attitude habitual, we are dealing with a case essentially the same as the one we have just considered. We are dealing with a disintegration of personality. He becomes the victim of every passing impulse and we can no longer treat him as a person but can only study him as an object.

It should now be evident that reason in practical affairs depends for its very intelligibility on an implicit logic of the passions, which depends in its turn on the teleology of the whole organism, this obviously being the product of nature and not of our reasoning itself. The view is entirely in line with Hume's naturalism. Nevertheless he is in conflict with it at a number of points. The reason lies in his treating the passions as mechanical rather than as teleological in their workings. This is seen in its extreme form in his discussion of the above cases, for he there treats passion and reason not simply as distinguishable but as entirely unrelated. Thus my passion is a fact about me on a level with my being more than five foot in height. In short, it is entirely unrelated to thought. His official view is that reason is subordinate to passion. This implies a relation. For example, reason assists a passion in finding its object. But even that relation he cannot explain, so long as he works on mechanistic assumptions. To see this, let us take those assumptions seriously. Suppose, for example, that the thought of an insult works as a mechanical cause in producing anger. The difficulty is to explain why the anger is affected later simply by a change in thought. Suppose you use your hands to push an object down a slope. You cannot affect its later motion simply by changing the position of your hands.

It is evident that the passions can be properly understood only when they are seen in their teleological relation to the whole person, and the person in his relation to the world. Moreover, Hume's naturalism requires precisely this view. To see this, we have only to recollect that he extends his view of the relation between reason and passion to cover also our reasoning about matters of fact. Here, too, reason depends finally on passion. Thus all reasoning about matters of fact depends on the idea of causality. But that idea arises from the *feeling* of certainty which is immediately occasioned by regularity. Regularity is a surface phenomenon. Hume insists that we have no rational insight into the nature of causality. Nevertheless, on the basis of feeling we are able to reason about matters of fact and accurately predict the course of nature. This view is incoherent unless we suppose that feeling is adjusted both to reason and to the world. The relation can hardly be accidental, for it is impossible to believe that as a matter of accident we continually anticipate the course of nature. In short, we are bound to assume that the relation of feeling both to reason and to the world involves some form of teleology or, as Hume called it, finality.

Now on the issue of finality, Hume, as usual, is inconsistent. In a letter to Hutcheson he rejected the idea of final causes and criticized Hutcheson for adopting it. Yet he himself presupposes the idea at innumerable points in the *Treatise*. He makes it plausible, for example, that our fundamental ideas are independent of reason by telling us that nature has not trusted matters of such importance to our fallible reasonings. Here Hume treats the relation between nature and the mind as purposive. Moreover, it is idle to dismiss this as a literary flourish, for the very coherence of his philosophy depends on there being some relation between ourselves and the world which is prior to reasoning but which cannot be explained in purely mechanical terms. Moreover in the *Enquiries* he more or less explicitly connects the idea of causality with that of finality.

> Here, then, is a kind of pre-established harmony between the course of nature and the succession of our ideas; and though the powers and forces by which the former is governed be wholly unknown to us, yet our thoughts and conceptions have still, we find, gone in the same train with the other works of nature.... Those who delight in the discovery and contemplation of *final causes* have here ample subject to employ their wonder and admiration.[12]

We must now pursue our theme into Book III, where Hume considers the nature of morality.

7

REASON AND MORALITY

Book III opens with a theme which follows easily from Hume's discussion of the passions. He takes as his object of attack the view that morality is derived from reason.[1]

> Those who affirm that virtue is nothing but a conformity to reason, that there are eternal fitnesses and unfitnesses of things, which are the same to every rational being that considers them; that the immutable measures of right and wrong impose an obligation, not only on human creatures but also on the Deity himself: All these systems concur in the opinion, that morality, like truth, is discern'd merely by ideas, and by their juxta–position and comparison. In order, therefore, to judge of these systems, we need only consider, whether it be possible, from reason alone to distinguish betwixt moral good and evil, or whether there must concur some other principle to enable us to make that distinction.[2]

This view, sometimes termed the deontological, is one of the two which have been most prominent in moral philosophy during the last few centuries. The other is the utilitarian. It will be useful for a moment to consider these two views, for we shall then see how Hume stands in relation to them. The deontological view is expressed in an extreme form by Kant. He held that the only good is a good will. A will is good when it is moved purely by a respect for duty. Respect for duty shows itself in a respect for law. Respect for law is respect for reason. An act, so far as it is morally pure, will therefore express in particular circumstances what is required by the very idea of reason or law. That is why the person who is morally pure will seek to will only what can be willed by any rational agent in those circumstances. But he can do this only by following his *own* reason. He cannot do so by conformity to the will of others. This applies even to the will of God. No act is good because God wills it. God wills it because it is good. Morality therefore is nothing but a conformity to reason which is the same for all rational beings and imposes itself not simply as human creatures but on the Deity himself.

Kant's views on moral philosophy show how greatly he was influenced by the idea of reason which flourished at the time of the enlightenment. They can hardly be explained by the influence on him of his background in strict Protestantism. To the strict Protestant, or Calvinist, they would be in many respects abhorrent. For Kant treats reason and morality with a reverence which is due only to God. Thus God no less then the rational individual is subject to the demands of morality and reason, and the rational individual, no less then God, has access to those demands. This is to attribute to the rational individual that knowledge of good and evil which is represented in Genesis by the tree from which we are forbidden to eat.

Now Kant was advancing views of a type which had already been criticized in detail by Francis Hutcheson.[3] Hutcheson argued that the sense of good and evil cannot be identified with reason, nor can it be derived from it. Whenever we reason about values, a sense of value is already presupposed. For example, a person chooses one act rather than another because it promotes his own interest or happiness. But why does he pursue his own interest or happiness? We may say that this is the principle which moves him. But the principle merely describes what moves him. He is not moved by the principle itself.

> This proposition is indeed true, 'There is an *instinct* or *desire* fixed in his nature, determining him to pursue his own happiness'; but it is not this *reflection* on his own nature, or this *proposition* which excites or determines him, but the *instinct itself*. This is a truth, 'Rhubarb strengthens the stomach': But 'tis not a *proposition* that strengthens the stomach, but the *quality* in that medicine. The effect is not produced by the *propositions* showing the *cause*, but by the *cause* itself.[4]

We cannot reason unless we know what *counts* as reasonable or unreasonable. What counts as reasonable or unreasonable depends on our basic instincts and dispositions. These are the rails, as it were, along which our reasons run. The point applies as much in morals as in any other form of practical reasoning. The child acquires a sense of good or evil in the form of desire and aversion. Desires and aversions are developed or diversified according to reasoning in particular circumstances. But that reasoning always presupposes those desires and aversions, which are given to us by nature.

Hutcheson's development of this point in relation to theology is striking in that he employs a distinction which is virtually identical with one that Kant employs in the *Critique of Pure Reason*. Kant argues, for example, that causality is relative to a phenomenal perspective. It is not subjective or illusory and must therefore have some base in the world which is independent of that perspective. It does not follow, however, that this base must *itself* be causal. It does not follow that causality must apply to the world in itself. Hutcheson employs a similar distinction to cover value. We may take as an instance the sense of beauty. This is not subjective in the sense of arising wholly from the subject. Indeed, that is not true even of our simplest tastes. I taste sugar and find it sweet. As Hutcheson says, I could not find it otherwise even if it were in my interest to do so. The taste is related to its object and that related to nature more generally. Even in experiencing the simplest taste I am but one element in a relation for which I am certainly not responsible myself. Similarly, as Hutcheson shows, our sense of beauty, however it may be developed by training, presupposes natural relations which are not the product of the individual will. Our pleasure in beauty, since it depends on relations which arise from the natural world, may be said to have its source in God. *It does not follow, however, that for God himself there is beauty in what thus pleases us.* The point becomes obvious, for example, if one recollects that the sense of beauty in the human form varies according to sexual differences and would vary even more strikingly across the species. It is then obvious that the sense of beauty is not absolute. Manifestly it is relative to the conditions imposed on us by our nature and cannot apply in the same form outside those conditions. Nor does the point apply only to aesthetic value. It is even more evident in the case of morals. Courage, for example, is a virtue because fear is endemic in the species and can be overcome only by an effort. Generosity is a virtue because self-interest is similarly endemic. It now becomes not so much false as absurd to suppose that these virtues are imposed in the same form on God. In this way, Hutcheson preserves the strict Protestant or Calvinist view that God is transcendent and that there is an impiety in supposing he can be measured by our own concepts.

The utilitarian view, though it differs greatly from Kant's, resembles it in seeking to base morality on reason. Bentham, the originator of utilitarianism, was influenced by the development of modern science and especially by the progress it had made in quantifying the processes of nature.[5] A difference between two things is quantitative when they differ only in the amount of what they otherwise have in common. The difference between an 8 lb and a 12 lb bag of potatoes is quantitative. The 12 lb bag contains more of what is contained in the other bag. But nature seems to present us with differences that are qualitative as well as quantitative. The difference between two colours, such as red and blue, would be an example. The difference seems not to be that blue contains more of what is contained in red, or red more of what is contained in blue. They just seem different. But in fact one can express the difference in quantitative terms, so long as one finds a neutral term. Thus physicists speak of colour in terms of light waves. Red and blue are light waves which differ in frequency and that for a physicist expresses the difference between them. In short, the difference is quantitative. Once a difference becomes quantitative, it can be expressed by a number. In other words, the processes of nature can be expressed in mathematical terms and this enormously increases the ability to predict and control them.

Bentham adopted the same procedure in dealing with morality. On the face of it, good and evil, like red and blue, differ in quality. But Bentham expressed their difference by means of a neutral term, pleasure. He argued that a good act differs from a bad in that it *increases* the sum of human pleasure or happiness. The difference is quantitative. It can also be expressed in terms of pain. A good act differs from a bad in that it *decreases* the sum of human pain or misery. The difference is still quantitative. Calculation can now replace argument. To determine which is the better of two acts one has only to calculate their consequences. That act is the better which produces the greater amount of pleasure or happiness. Morality is now based on reason.

That, of course, is to presuppose that goodness really is equivalent to pleasure. Bentham argued that this must be so, since all action is directed towards pleasure. A fortiori moral action must be thus directed. He did not mean that there is no important difference, for example, between the selfish and the generous. A selfish person gets his pleasure from helping himself; a generous person from helping others. Nevertheless, they have the same end and differ only over the means to achieve it. It follows that all differences in value must be differences over how to achieve a common end. But then it follows also that this common end provides us with a criterion external to the differences themselves by which they can be assessed. In short, the principle of utility, of what produces the greater pleasure, will enable us on purely rational ground to remove all disagreements over value.

Now Bentham, also, was advancing views which had already been criticized in detail by Hutcheson. Thus, for Hutcheson, pleasure is an aspect of value, not an end which confers value on everything else. For that reason, where values differ it cannot serve as a criterion external to them. Suppose, for example, I take pleasure in music. It cannot be the pleasure which gives value to the music, since if I did not already value the music it would not give me pleasure. Money can confer value on a job. For even if a person hates the job he can still do it simply for the money. But plainly if he hates music he cannot listen to it simply for the pleasure it gives him. Indeed it is evident that the pleasure a person takes in music is the sign of how much he values it. Now suppose I take pleasure in music and you hate it. It is not that we share a common end and differ simply in how to achieve it. We simply differ in what we value. Thus the pleasure in my case, the displeasure in yours, are the signs of what we value, not their measure.

As Hutcheson insists, pleasure is a secondary end; it arises through the satisfaction of a passion which is not directed at pleasure. Consequently, one cannot *simply* aim at pleasure, for one attains pleasure by aiming at something else. For that reason, the generous and the selfish do not differ simply over the means they adopt to achieve the same aim. The generous person's aim is not to obtain his own pleasure but to help others. He takes pleasure in helping others because he *wants* to help them. Therefore in taking pleasure he shows how much he values the others, not himself. By contrast, the selfish person shows how much he values himself, not the others. In short, their aims are not at all the same.

In their primary form all the passions are disinterested. They aim at their object not at the self. Thus one eats not because it is in one's interest but because one desires food. That is why a person who loses the desire for food finds it almost impossible to eat, though he knows it is in his interest. Self-interest arises not through the workings of passion in itself but through its conflict with other passions, as when, for example, you can satisfy your own desire for food only at the expense of someone else. Self-love arises only when you can distinguish yourself from others, as when, for example, others receive the praise you would like yourself. But even self-love is different from calculated self-interest and is often in conflict with it. For example, a proud man will sacrifice his own interest, or even risk his life, in order to avenge an insult.

It is true of course that a person's interest is promoted through the workings of his passions. But that is through a marvellous teleology whereby the passions promote in combination what none pursues individually. There is an analogy with the organs of the body. The function of the eye is not to preserve the whole organism but to see; the function of the ear to hear; and so on. Nevertheless, the various organs are so interrelated that they preserve the whole organism simply by performing their own function. Similarly, it is not the function of appetite to preserve the whole person but to obtain food. Nevertheless, through obtaining food it helps to preserve the whole person. This teleology is evidently not the product of human reasoning. Such reasoning is merely an aspect of the teleology. For example, the purpose of calculated self-interest is to correct an excess in the functioning of the passions, as when the thought of the consequences restrains your anger. It is noticeable, however, that the calculation of self-interest works only when there is already a certain level of integration amongst the passions. As we have said, unrestrained pride will scorn self-interest.

Thus, against a rationalist view of morality, whether of the deontological or the utilitarian type, Hutcheson advances a thoroughgoing naturalism. Morality arises not from reason alone but through a natural teleology of which human reasoning itself is a mere aspect. Moreover, we have dwelt on Hutcheson's views because they form the basis for Hume's. It is true that in Hume there is a somewhat greater emphasis on utilitarian reasoning. Some have even classified him as a utilitarian. But that is certainly mistaken. Hume insists that calculations about the general happiness, though they have a place in morality, always presuppose, in order to be effective, the passion of benevolence, which cannot itself be derived from such calculation. To see this in detail, however, we must turn to Hume's own account.

As we have said, Hume's object of attack is the view that morality is derived from reason. He has already shown, in Book II, that reason alone cannot move the will. He next argues that morality is essentially connected with the will. It is primarily concerned not with what is the case but with what one ought to do. His conclusion now easily follows. If morality is essentially connected with the will and reason alone cannot move the will, reason alone cannot be the basis of morality.

In support of this view, Hume repeats some of his earlier points. He repeats the claim, for example, that a passion can be called unreasonable only where it is associated with a false belief about its object or about the means to satisfy it. But, he continues, false belief is plainly not equivalent to moral wrong. For example, a murderer may be correct both in identifying his object and in the means he adopts to achieve his end. But that does not make him any less evil. He is evil not in his beliefs but in the passion that moves him. By contrast, if a man miscalculates in seeking to help another, we tend to excuse rather than to blame him, because his passion is good. Consequently the difference between good and evil cannot be equivalent to being reasonable or unreasonable in one's beliefs.

Hume now considers whether morality can be derived from reasoning of the a priori or demonstrative type. This type of reasoning depends simply on the relations that hold between ideas. Thus from the idea of a bachelor one can infer that any bachelor is unmarried. Can one similarly infer from the very idea of an action that such an action is morally wrong? For example, the idea of patricide implies that of being killed by one's off-spring. Does the very idea of being killed by one's off-spring imply that such an act is morally wrong? Hume argues that if one simply considers the relation involved, this does not follow. He supports this view by the following argument.

> To put the affair, therefore, to this trial, let us chuse any inanimate object, such as an oak or elm; and let us suppose, that by the dropping of its seed, it produces a sapling below it, which springing up by degrees, at last overtops and destroys the parent tree: I ask, if in this instance there be wanting any relation, which is discoverable in patricide or ingratitude? Is not the one tree the cause of the other's existence; and the latter the cause of the destruction of the former, in the same manner as when a child murders his parent? 'Tis not sufficient to reply that a choice or will is wanting. For in the case of patricide, a will does not give rise to any *different* relations, but is only the cause from which the action is deriv'd; and consequently produces the *same* relations, that in the oak or elm arise from some other principles. 'Tis a will or choice, that determines a man to kill his parents; and they are the laws of matter and motion, that determine a sapling to destroy the oak, from which it sprung. Here then the same relations have different causes, but still the relations are the same: And as their discovery is not in both cases attended with a notion of immorality, it follows, that that notion does not arise from such a discovery.[6]

Now this surely is a very dubious argument. The sapling does not know that it kills its parent, nor even that it kills. In the human sphere, the nearest parallel is with a child that kills by accident a person it does not know is its parent. But we should no more blame the child than we should the sapling. It is obvious, however, that Hume would treat this point as irrelevant. For him, the relation involved in killing a parent is an external event which must be characterized independently of the agent that produces it. That is why it can be produced as readily by a sapling as by a human being. The human being has knowledge and will, but these are relevant only to the agent, which is the cause, not to the act, which is an effect, and therefore quite distinct. Here we see, yet again, the influence on Hume's philosophy of mechanistic assumptions. It is absurd to suppose that the sapling and the human being do the same thing and differ only in how they come to do it. For the concepts of doing something are different. Thus one cannot distinguish a human action from the belief and intention of the agent, since without belief and intention one has not yet arrived at the level of human action.

It is true, of course, that there are many relations which are unaffected by intention and belief. Whether there is a hole in my pocket does not depend on whether I know it is there or on what I intend to do about it. But the relations involved in human action are precisely not of this type. What I do depends for its character on what I intend and that upon what I know or believe. Suppose, for example, that someone is thirsty and I get him water. Then I discover that the water is poisoned. I can no longer do what I intend, for I know that in giving him the water I shall kill him. Here what I do depends on what I intend and what I intend on what I know. For if I know the water is poisoned, I cannot intend and therefore cannot perform the act of simply relieving his thirst.

Hume, however, draws upon other considerations to support his view about the relation between reason and morality.

> Take any action allowed to be vicious: Wilful murder, for instance. Examine it in all lights, and see if you can find that matter of fact, or real existence, which you call *vice*. In which-ever way you take it, you find only certain passions, motives, volitions and thoughts. There is no other matter of fact in the case. The vice entirely escapes you, as long as you consider the object. For you can never find it, till you turn your reflexion into your own breast, and find a sentiment of disapprobation, which arises in you, towards this action. Here is a matter of fact but 'tis the object of feeling, not of reason. It lies in yourself, not in the object. So that when you pronounce any action or character to be vicious, you mean nothing, but that from the constitution of your nature you have a feeling or sentiment of blame from the contemplation of it.[7]

If we exclude every element of personal attitude from the description of a murder we are left with a neutral description rather than a moral judgement. Consequently, in expressing a moral judgement, one's own attitude is an essential element, and this cannot depend on reason alone. The trouble with the above passage, however, is that the moral attitude is conveyed in excessively subjectivist terms. Hume treats the disapproval of murder on the model of a sensation and its cause. Suppose, for example, that I feel heat and note that the radiators are too hot. In a similar way, according to Hume, I feel sensations of disapproval in my breast and note the murder as their cause. Now I do not have to know the radiators are too hot before feeling the heat. Indeed, it is usually through feeling the heat that I know the radiators are too high. It is absurd, however, to suppose that in disapproving of murder I first feel sensations of disapproval and only later discover that someone has been murdered. It is only through my belief about the murder that my disapproval is intelligible. The very point of my moral judgement is to convey, not that I feel *this*, but that given the character of the act it is only this one can *appropriately* feel. My judgement about what is appropriate to the act is evidently unintelligible unless I am already aware of it. Thus in condemning an act as murder I seek to judge the act, not to describe my own feelings. It is true that in condemning the murder I convey my own attitude but I do this by judging the act, not by talking about myself. It is evident also that any moral judgement will involve, if only implicitly, some element of reasoning. Hume, by contrast, gives the impression that the two are not simply distinguishable but are entirely separate. Moral disapproval, in short, has nothing at all to do with reason. As we shall see, however, Hume later corrects this impression.

We now come to one of the most famous passages in the *Treatise*. It will be useful to quote it in full.

> I cannot forbear adding to these reasonings an observation, which may, perhaps, be found of some importance. In every system of morality, which I have hitherto met with, I have always remark'd that the author proceeds for some time in the ordinary way of reasoning, and establishes the being of God, or makes observations concerning human affairs; when of a sudden I am surpriz'd to find, that instead of the usual copulations of propositions *is* and *is not*, I meet with no proposition that is not connected with an *ought* or an *ought not*. This change is imperceptible; but is, however, of the last consequence. For as this *ought* or *ought not* expresses some new relation or affirmation, 'tis necessary that it shou'd be observ'd and explain'd; and at the same time that a reason should be given, for what seems altogether inconceivable, how this new relation can be a deduction from others, which are entirely different from it. But as authors do not commonly use this precaution, I shall presume to recommend it to the readers; and am persuaded that this small attention wou'd subvert all the

vulgar systems of morality, and let us see, that the distinction of vice and virtue is not founded merely on the relations of objects, nor is perceived by reason.[8]

Few passages in Hume's philosophy have been quoted more often than this one. Here we have Hume's so-called distinction between fact and value. It is noticeable that he does not himself employ those terms. He distinguishes between 'is' and 'ought' statements and he claims that many philosophers move from the one to the other without justifying their transition between the two. He does *seem* to claim that no such transition *can* be justified. I stress 'seem' because it is not clear whether or not he is simply making a literary flourish. Many, however, have held that he was making this claim and have held also that he was correct to do so. According to these philosophers, fact and value are not simply separable but logically unrelated, so that any movement between the two can depend only on choice or will, these being arbitrary with regard to fact. This view was common, for example, to the logical positivists and to the existentialists.[9] We shall consider this view later. First, we must consider what in the above passage is Hume's primary intention.[10]

Suppose a person says 'Immigrants *are* increasing so we *ought* to restrict their entry'. Plainly, if I do not mind an increase in the number of immigrants, I can accept the factual premise in this argument whilst denying its evaluative conclusion. In short, the conclusion of the argument does not follow if its premise is purely factual. It requires the further suppressed evaluative premise 'Immigrants ought not to increase in number'. Moreover, it seems evident that the point can be generalized. No evaluative conclusion can follow from a premise which is purely factual. The point seems evident because by a purely factual premise we mean one which, in itself, has no evaluative implications. If a premise has no evaluative implications, it cannot entail an evaluative conclusion.

Now Hume's prime intention, in the passage we have quoted, is to show the relevance of the above point in considering those philosophers who seek to base the distinction between good and evil on pure reason or a bare relation between objects; who wish, in short, to derive morality from a purely factual premise. His point is that if their premise is purely factual, it cannot sustain their conclusion; if it appears to sustain their conclusion, that is because it is not purely factual but contains a suppressed evaluative assumption. We may illustrate his point by returning to the two philosophers we considered earlier.

Bentham claims that morality is based on the principle of the greatest happiness. Moreover, he certainly gives the impression that one can arrive at this principle simply through rational analysis, without already being committed to some principle itself evaluative. But the principle enjoins that we *ought* to pursue the general happiness. It is itself evaluative. Indeed, it is not simply evaluative but also controversial. Many have claimed, for example, that happiness is less important than justice and that where the two are in conflict we should promote justice not happiness. In short, Bentham has not arrived at his principle through pure reason; he has merely emphasized one moral principle in preference to others. Consequently, one can arrive at his conclusion only if one accepts also the suppressed, and so far unjustified, evaluative assumption that the most important of all moral principles is the one he favours.

Kant affirms that morality follows from the principle of universalisability. Thus in order to determine what act is morally right, it is sufficient to determine what act in the circumstances can be willed by all rational agents. Here it seems that evaluative conclusions may be derived from a principle which contains in itself no evaluative content. They seem to be the mere consequence of acting with rational consistency. But this is an illusion. Without assuming some evaluative content the principle cannot be applied. This becomes obvious when one realizes that incompatible moral views may both satisfy the principle. Suppose I claim that the death penalty should be abolished and you deny this. We may each affirm without contradiction that our proposal should be willed by all rational agents. Rational consistency may be a necessary condition for arriving at an evaluative conclusion, but it is not a sufficient one. It follows that one cannot arrive at an evaluative conclusion on the basis of rational consistency alone.

Hume's point, then, is that philosophers who seek to base morality purely on reason sustain their view by a fallacious transition from fact to value. He is not, of course, claiming that they make this move of deliberate intent. They may themselves be deceived. His point is that we should be alert to detect the fallacy. The fallacy, when isolated, is obvious. Thus it is obvious that a purely factual statement cannot imply an evaluative conclusion, since by a purely factual statement we mean one which has no such implications. Thus the statement that immigrants are increasing in number may be taken as purely factual, because it carries an evaluative implication, not in itself, but only when it is related to other facts and some evaluative attitude. The point of drawing our attention to this obvious truth is simply that in practice it is often overlooked.

Let us now consider how Hume's point has been taken in the present century. As we have said, it has been taken to show that fact and value are entirely separate. It follows not simply that the transition between the two is sometimes or often unjustified. On the view we are now considering, no such transition can ever be justified in rational terms but depends only on choice or will. If I dislike immigrants, the increase in their number will have for me evaluative implications. If you like them, it will also for you have evaluative implications, but of an exactly opposite type. The relation between the fact and the differing evaluations is not based on reason but simply on personal attitude. Thus, ultimately, value is arbitrary with regard to fact, and where the two are related the relation is arbitrary with regard to reason. This view was advanced, as we have said, by the existentialists and in Britain by the logical positivists. Later philosophers, such as R. M. Hare, adopted what was essentially the same view, though Hare attempted to introduce into it some element of reason by arguing that once a value is chosen one is bound in consistency to apply it in the same way in all relevant circumstances.[11]

Now the above view, which is adopted by the existentialists and the logical positivists, rests on a fallacy. They have assumed that because the factual may be separated from the evaluative, what is evaluative cannot be factual. This is like assuming that because being British can be separated from being Welsh, a man who is Welsh cannot be British. Contrary to what they have assumed, there are many facts which are already evaluative. A sensation such as pain will serve as an example. I experience pain as something *awful*. I do not experience it as a pure fact and then project upon it an attitude of awfulness. I cannot separate the awfulness from the pain. Pain is certainly a fact but it is an *awful* one. It may be said that this view is refuted by the existence of masochists, who delight in pain. But their delight in pain is rendered intelligible by their associating it with something else, such as sexual arousal and therefore sexual pleasure. The difference between a masochist and myself cannot be that when the dentist drills into an exposed nerve, the masochist feels *exactly* what I do, except he happens to like it. For then I should not find him intelligible at all. I should not find him intelligible, because I cannot even conceive of such a pain apart from its awfulness.

The same point applies to feelings which are slightly more complicated. For example, a hungry person wants food, which is to say that he values it. But could he *not* value it and still be in a state of hunger? Again, to make this intelligible you have to bring in extra facts, such as his knowing the food is poisoned. Otherwise you cannot separate his attitude from his state. Exactly the same point applies to moral value. Suppose someone's hunger arouses my compassion. I feel I ought to give him food. What I ought to do is already implicit in my compassion. That I am in this state is a fact. But it is a fact from which it follows for me that I ought to help the other. This does not mean that I *infer* this, from noting I am in this state. I cannot feel compassion without feeling that I ought to help. The feeling is *already* evaluative. In feeling, fact and value meet. Here values are grounded in facts. Thus in feeling or desire, fact and value may be distinguished but they cannot be separated. Without the evaluative element there is no desire; without the fact that it occurs there is no evaluative element to contemplate.

The above points become obvious once one recognizes that feelings or emotions involve a natural teleology. They involve a direction and goal and therefore a value. To be hungry is to have food as one's goal. In short, one values food. To be compassionate is to have one's interest directed towards another. In short, the other becomes interesting, an object of value. For that reason, emotion cannot be arbitrary with regard to fact. One cannot feel compassion for a stone wall. The emotion has as its object the relief of suffering or of some harm. Inside that context, one may feel compassion. Outside, nothing counts as such. By the same token, the objects of pride or anger cannot be whatever one happens to choose. One feels anger at being insulted but not pride, and pride at one's own achievements but not anger. The emotions have an implicit logic or teleology which cannot be based on human choice or will. It is true that value cannot rest on *pure* reason or *pure* fact, for these are not the kinds of fact or reason which are relevant to value. But it does not follow that value is arbitrary with regard to reason or fact. Quite the contrary, value has its base in a natural teleology, which is manifest in the workings of the emotions.

Hume has now established, at least to his own satisfaction, that morality is not based simply on reason. He proceeds to summarize his view. Here, we may note, he begins to correct the impression of extreme subjectivism which he conveyed earlier.

> An action, or sentiment, or character is virtuous or vicious; Why? because its view causes a pleasure or uneasiness of a particular kind. In giving a reason, therefore, for the pleasure or uneasiness, we sufficiently explain the vice or virtue. To have the sense of virtue, is nothing but to *feel* a satisfaction of a particular kind from the contemplation of a character. The very *feeling* constitutes our praise or admiration. We go no further; nor do we enquire into the cause of the satisfaction. We do not infer a character to be virtuous, because it pleases: But in feeling that it pleases after such a particular manner, we in effect feel that it is virtuous. The case is the same as in our judgements concerning all kinds of beauty, and tastes, and sensations. Our approbation is imply'd in the immediate pleasure they convey to us.[12]

The first sentence in the above quotation seems to reinforce the impression of subjectivism. An action is virtuous or vicious because of the pleasure or uneasiness it gives. This may seem like my reason for calling it virtuous or vicious. It is virtuous or vicious because of the pleasure or uneasiness it gives *me*. Hume makes clear, however, that this is not really his view. His view in fact is identical with Hutcheson's. I do not *infer* that the action is virtuous because I note in myself pleasure or approval. My pleasure or approval is directed towards the action. It is the action I find good, not the effect it produces in myself. Here, at least implicitly, Hume recognizes the intentional nature of the emotions. The value of the object is not derived from the pleasure it gives. It would not give me pleasure unless I found it valuable. Thus in my pleasure or approval I *already* acknowledge the value of the object. I do not need to infer it later from what is occurring in myself.

Hume proceeds to remove still further the impression of subjectivism. He recognizes that 'pleasure' is not adequate as an equivalent for 'approval'. We find pleasure in many things of which, in the moral sense, we do not approve and approve of many things in which, in the normal sense, we do not find pleasure. How is this to be explained?

> The good qualities of an enemy are hurtful to us; but may still command our esteem and respect. 'Tis only when a character is considered in general, without reference to our particular interest, that it causes such a feeling or sentiment, as denominates it morally good or evil.[13]

We have already said that someone who expresses a moral judgement does not seek to draw attention to his own personal feelings. Certainly he expresses those feelings but he does so in a particular form. He expresses them in the form of *what it is appropriate to feel*. There is, in short, a certain generality or impersonality about a moral judgement which distinguishes it, for example, from the expression of a preference. If I express a preference for coffee over tea I do not thereby imply that my attitude is the only appropriate one. This is the point which Hume acknowledges in the above passage. He thereby acknowledges also, if only implicitly, that reason is essential to morality and not its accidental accompaniment. Without some power of reflection, for example, whereby he can distinguish what is personal from what has general significance, the child will never develop a sense of morality. Reason is not the basis of morality but it is one of its essential elements.

Hume ends Part I by stating a topic he will deal with in detail in Part II. To what extent does morality depend on propensities inherent in our nature and to what extent on social circumstance? The question has a point because Hume takes for granted that not all our moral duties can be explained simply by natural propensity.

> For as the number of our duties is, in a manner, infinite, 'tis impossible that our original instincts should extend to each of them....Such a method of proceeding is not conformable to the usual maxims, by which nature is conducted, where a few principles produce all that variety we observe in the universe, and every thing is carry'd on in the easiest and most simple manner.[14]

As we have said, Hume will deal with this topic in the next part of Book III but he prepares the way by distinguishing three senses of the word natural.

1   The natural may be distinguished from the miraculous, that which does from that which does not form part of the system of nature. In this sense morality is natural.

2   The natural may be contrasted with the abnormal, what is customary with what is remarkable or rare. In this sense, also, morality may be said to be natural enough.

3   Natural may be contrasted with what Hume calls the artificial, what we may call nurture. Here there arises a real question, since it is not easy to determine how much morality depends on nurture or social training and how much on original endowment. It is already obvious however that *both* these factors will figure in Hume's account.

Nature and artifice

The second part of Book III, which deals with the nature of justice, constitutes one of Hume's most brilliant and original contributions to philosophy. To get the measure of his achievement, we must consider the type of view against which he is implicitly arguing. In social philosophy, especially of the empiricist type, there has been a persistent tendency to explain social institutions as devices for satisfying desires or needs which exist independently of them. Bentham, for example, insisted that society is simply a collection of individuals and is therefore to be understood by understanding the individuals which comprise it. The method is comparable with that of the physical scientist. A chemist, for example, breaks down a substance into its component parts, analyses the nature of the parts and then, through bringing them together again, understands the nature of the substance. In a similar way, individuals are taken in abstraction from society, their nature analysed and society explained as what results when the individuals who have this nature come together. This method is common to the social contract theorists. Hobbes, for example, assumes a state of nature, in which individuals live quite independently of social bonds, each pursuing his interest in conflict with the others.[15] Society arises as a device by which they can be delivered from this state of perpetual warfare. They enter social existence by surrendering their rights to a sovereign, who has the power to keep them in peace. Here society is explained as a device by which essentially war-like creatures can be preserved from their own destructiveness. Social contract theories differ in their details but they have a common pattern. First, individuals are portrayed as they exist *before* they enter society. Then they enter society by calculating that it will bring them benefits they cannot obtain without it.

Now Hume, by contrast, argues that the benefits of society can be calculated only by those who *already* have some experience of it. Consequently it cannot have arisen as a result of such a calculation. For Hume, the idea that society could have arisen through a contract is simply a myth. Indeed such an idea not only lacks historical support but is incoherent in its details, for it attributes to individuals in a state of nature attitudes and procedures which presuppose the social life they are supposed to explain. Hobbes, for example, assumes that individuals in a state of nature form a contract with their sovereign by which they surrender their rights in exchange for his protection. But these procedures presuppose a sense of justice which can develop only *within* social life. Thus Hume argues that justice is artificial. By this he means that it cannot arise in a state of nature but only through the calculations of individuals who are already interested in a social life of whose benefits they are aware. Consequently, society cannot be based on calculations about the general interest. Rather such calculations arise only through developments in society itself.

In fact, Hume, as usual, is inconsistent. In describing justice as an artifice, he implies that it arises through conscious contrivance. As we shall see, it does not at all arise through conscious contrivance, though it may involve such contrivances once it has arisen. Justice presupposes an interrelation of individual natures but it is not consciously developed or designed by the individuals thus interrelated. A thoroughgoing naturalism would recognize that justice is an outgrowth of nature rather than a product of calculation. But this is an inconsistency in the way Hume develops a point which itself is brilliant and remarkable. In emphasizing the social over the individual, he anticipated that shift in historical and social thinking which is characteristic of the nineteenth century rather than of his own. To see this in detail, let us turn to his account.

Hume's starting point is the same as Kant's. He argues that the goodness of an act depends on its motive. Thus we do not praise the person who helps another, if his motive is self-interested; nor do we blame a person who fails to help another, if he tries and his motive is generous. In his development of this point, however, Hume is directly opposed to Kant. If the goodness of an act depends on its motive, we may inquire wherein lies the goodness of the motive. Hume replies that it cannot lie in a respect for goodness itself. He does not deny that this can be a motive. But it cannot be primary. In other words, a respect for goodness itself (or virtue, or duty) can arise only as a secondary motive which is parasitic on others not themselves directed at goodness. Thus we praise a parent for doing his duty when he cares for his children. But his primary motive is to care for his children, not to do his duty. He need not be thinking of his duty at all. Moreover, we say he has done his duty because we value the care of children. We do not value the care of children *because* it is a duty. Again, this is not to deny that duty can be a motive. For example, a parent who has little natural affection for his children may still seek to care for them, because he reminds himself it is a duty. In fact, however, he seems a *worse* rather than a *better* parent than the one who cares for his children, without thinking of his duty, simply because he loves them. Hume gives other examples.

> Here is a man, that does many benevolent actions; relieves the distress'd, comforts the afflicted, and extends his bounty even to the greatest strangers. No character can be more amiable and virtuous.

We regard these actions as proofs of the greatest humanity. This humanity bestows a merit on the actions. A regard to this merit is, therefore, a secondary consideration, and deriv'd from an antecedent principle of humanity, which is meritorious and laudable.[16]

Hume now concludes as follows.

In short, it may be establish'd as an undoubted maxim, *that no action can be virtuous, or morally good unless there be in human nature some motive to produce it, distinct from the sense of its morality.*[17]

He emphasizes, once again, that he is not denying that morality or virtue may on some occasions be the sole motive for an action.

When any virtuous motive or principle is common in human nature, a person, who feels his heart devoid of that principle, may hate himself upon that account, and may perform the action without the motive, from a certain sense of duty, in order to acquire by practice, that virtuous principle, or at least, to disguise in himself, as much as possible, his want of it....But tho', on some occasions, a person may perform an action merely out of regard to its moral obligation, yet still this supposes in human nature some distinct principles, which are capable of producing the action, and whose moral beauty renders the action meritorious.[18]

Hume now considers justice. By this he means equity in our dealings with others. There are certain actions which are due to any person, irrespective of personal tie. For example, I have borrowed ten pounds from a man and have promised to repay it. The money is due to the man. Hume's aim is to find the primary motive in such a case. Why ought I to repay the ten pounds? Here it will not do to say I ought to repay it because I have promised. For a promise is what I *ought* to keep. In other words, in appealing to the promise we are appealing to duty. But Hume has already shown that duty cannot be a primary motive. To see the point, we have only to return to a previous example. In caring for his children a parent does his duty. But we call this a duty because we value the natural affection he shows in doing so. In short, caring for one's children is a duty because there is a motive to do so which we value independently of duty itself. Now what is the equivalent motive in the case of keeping a promise? What natural affection does it reveal which we so value that we call it a duty? The answer cannot be that in keeping a promise we do our duty.

Hume's argument is that in the case of justice there is no natural motive or affection. That is why he calls it an artificial virtue. To establish his case, he considers what natural motive or affection might be relevant. Self-interest seems evidently not relevant. Justice is preeminently the virtue which benefits the other person, not oneself. For that reason, however, the relevant motive may seem to be benevolence. Hume readily acknowledges that this motive is natural. Social training can encourage but can hardy implant a kindly feeling towards others. Hume denies, however, that justice is based on this feeling. In this, he seems evidently correct. For example, my duty to keep a promise to this person does not depend on my having kindly feelings towards him. My promise, once made, ought to be kept, whatever I feel about him. Nor do you have to feel kindly towards that person before condemning me for not keeping my promise. Moreover, benevolence, though real, is severely limited.

> In general, it may be affirm'd, that there is no such passion in human minds, as the love of mankind, merely as such, independent of personal qualities, of services, or of relation to oneself. 'Tis true, there is no human, and indeed no sensible, creature, whose happiness or misery does not, in some measure, affect us, when brought near to us, and represented in lively colours: But this proceeds merely from sympathy, and is no proof of such an universal affection to mankind, since this concern extends itself beyond our own species.[19]

We feel sympathy for any creature where we are vividly aware of its happiness or misery. But that results from our sympathy with the happiness or misery not from our love of mankind. Thus we feel such sympathy for animals as well as for human beings. In any case, we feel benevolence not for the whole of mankind but for those of its members who are brought vividly before us, and even for those only in particular circumstances. To those at a distance we are almost invariably indifferent. Hume might have gone further. Sympathy is one of the most divisive qualities. For it is readily occasioned in a group by their finding a common enemy. In short, it is readily occasioned by hatred and serves to stimulate the hatred which occasions it.

Hume therefore concludes that there is no natural motive or affection for justice. He then proceeds to give his own account of how justice arises. He begins by giving an account of how it arises in the case of property. Man, he says, is conspicuous amongst the animals in his need for a social life. He lacks the strength or speed of some and the modest needs of others. It is to the advantages of society that he owes his superiority.

> But in order to form society, 'tis requisite not only that it be advantageous, but also that men be sensible of its advantages; and 'tis impossible, in their wild and uncultivated state, that by study and reflection alone, they should ever be able to attain this knowledge.[20]

Society cannot have arisen because men calculated its benefits, for those benefits are known only by those who already know society. Consequently it must have arisen through motives and acts not directed towards it. Hume supposes it to have evolved from more primitive forms based on the family. Thus it is not the necessity for society but some other which gives rise to society itself.

> This necessity is no other than that natural appetite betwixt the sexes, which unites them together, and preserves their union, till a new tie takes place in their concern for their common offspring. Their new concern becomes also a principle of union betwixt the parents and offspring, and forms a more numerous society; where the parents govern by the advantage of their superior strength and wisdom, and at the same time are restrained in the exercise of their authority by that natural affection, which they bear their children.[21]

Once society has developed, men will readily be sensible of its benefits. But they will be sensible also of dangers to its stability. These arise especially from competition for a certain type of good. A contented mind and a healthy body are goods which can be destroyed but which cannot simply be transferred from one person to another. The same is not true of those possessions which we have obtained through industry or good fortune. If you take my plough, it is the same plough and it is as good for you as it is for me. This, of course, would cause no danger to society, were human beings moved entirely by benevolent instincts. It is evident, however, that their selfish instincts are at least as strong as their benevolent ones. You have motive enough to take my plough.

Now justice arises because human beings, aware of the dangers to society and sensible of its benefits, take steps to preserve the benefits by protecting themselves against the dangers. They institute a system of justice, according to which each individual is granted the right to his own property so long as he respects the property of others. That is why justice is artificial. It arises not from a natural motive or affection but as a tactic which we invent in order to preserve the benefits of society.

The details of the above procedure, however, are very obscure. At first, we take Hume to be claiming that the system of property arises through deliberate calculation and by explicit agreement. In short, it does not evolve from other forms but is instituted, at a given time and place, by all the members of the society who come together to preserve the interests of the society as a whole.

> For when men, from their early education in society, have become sensible of the infinite advantages that result from it...and when they have observ'd, that the principal disturbance in society arises from those goods which we call external...they must seek for a remedy....This can be done after no other manner, than by a

convention enter'd into by all the members of the society to bestow stability on the possession of these external goods, and leave every one in the peaceable enjoyment of what he may acquire by his fortune and industry.[22]

Now if justice has arisen as a result of such a procedure, we may well feel entitled to call it artificial. But it is impossible to believe that it has arisen as the result of such a procedure. We must remember that the people involved have, as yet, no sense of justice and no feeling for the general interest. They cannot have a sense of justice since this arises from the convention which, when they come together, they have not yet framed. They cannot have a feeling for the general interest, because, as Hume explicitly affirms, they are moved only by their own interest and that of their immediate circle. But then why should they trust one another? The difficulty becomes especially acute when one considers that justice, for Hume, arises in connection with property. Every system of property, known to us in history, reveals elements of inequality, some would say injustice, by which the majority are placed at a disadvantage over and against the few. It is not easy to believe that such a system has arisen in a society through the explicit agreement of all its members.

Within a page, however, we find that Hume has changed his tune.

> Two men, who pull the oars of a boat, do it by an agreement or convention, 'tho they have never given promises to each other. Nor is the rule concerning the stability of possession the less deriv'd from conventions, that it arises gradually, and acquires force by a slow progression, and by our repeated experience of the inconveniences of transgressing it.[23]

Here evolution has replaced explicit agreement. A property system now seems less a tactic or device than a product of natural growth. As this point, Hume's account becomes more plausible. Take by analogy the development of a free market system. The system develops through the transactions of individuals, each of whom seeks his or her own profit. In seeking this profit, each adjusts his or her manoeuvres to allow a similar profit to another. In this way there develops a complicated economic system. Hume's suggestion now seems to be that a property system arises through similar developments. But let us note that the system, by that very token, ceases to be a matter of artificial or conscious contrivance. The point is evident in our example from economics. In a free market system each individual consciously contrives to secure his own profit, not to develop the system. The system develops through the consequences of what each individual intends but those consequences are not themselves intended. In short, the system as a whole is not a conscious contrivance at all. The process, indeed, is no different in kind from the one which Hume, in opposition to the social contract theorists, attributes to society in its earlier developments. Just as it is other necessities which give rise to society and not the necessity for society itself, so it is not the necessity for the economic system itself but other necessities which give rise to the economic system.

But there is still a difficulty. There are extreme advocates of the free market system who speak of it in moral and even quasi-religious terms. But that is not an attitude which most of us find natural. Even those of us who are in favour of the system would hesitate to describe it as a system of justice. Moreover, the reason seems obvious. It is based on self-interest. In this case, self-interest may work to the benefit of society as a whole. But it is not the benefit of society as a whole which is the primary motive of those involved in the system. They pursue their own profit. Yet Hume has no better motive for justice. It arises through the mutual adjustments of self-interested parties. Later, he tries to meet this difficulty by arguing that the moral element arises through reflection. When we reflect on the system, its benefit for society is brought vividly before us and this, through stimulating our benevolent instincts, leads to our treating the system in moral terms. But few of us are inclined to treat our economic system in such terms, even though we believe that it benefits society.

Similar difficulties arise in Hume's treatment of promise-keeping. He holds, as we have seen, that in the case of promise-keeping there is no natural motive or affection to explain the obligation involved. He therefore argues that promises are human inventions founded on the necessities and interests of society.

The chief necessity arises through the limitations of human benevolence. If I help you now, when I can afford it, you may help me later, when you can afford it yourself. In this way, we both benefit. There is, however, a difficulty. If I help you now, your benefit is immediate and certain. My benefit is in the future and is perhaps conjectural. Moreover, you no longer have a motive to benefit me since you have already received your benefit. So why should I trust you? That, of course, is to assume that human beings are self-interested. A benevolent person will certainty return a benefit received. But unless you are one of my immediate circle I cannot trust your benevolence. So the difficulty remains.

Now Hume suggests that promise-keeping is an invention designed to overcome this difficulty. It is not easy, however, to see how the invention is supposed to work. If I cannot trust you to return a benefit, why should I trust you when you tell me that you will return it? But what if we all get together and agree that we shall benefit from trusting one another, and what if we ensure this by agreeing that if anyone does not return a benefit we shall all join in and blame him for breaking his word? The difficulty is that if we do not trust one another, we cannot trust one another to keep the agreement. Someone, after all, has to start. And then it is a matter of conjecture that he or she will be supported by those who agreed to do so. Promise-keeping might serve as the paradigm case of an institution that cannot have been based on utilitarian calculations. For the utilitarian benefits follow only given a widespread knowledge that the institution already exists. Unless there is *already* a widespread resentment against people who break their word, what is there in a mere promise to restrain self-interested people from breaking theirs? It is true that *legal* justice may be considered in some respects as an invention or device. Laws to enforce contract, for example, may be introduced through a calculation of their benefits. But laws work best where they reflect moral attitudes already existing in the community. Otherwise they can be enforced only by naked force. But such laws have no element of *moral* authority. It is evident, in short, that legal calculation can merely reflect moral authority; it cannot create it.

The nature of justice is one of the issues on which Hume and Hutcheson disagreed. Hutcheson insisted that justice has a natural base; Hume insisted that it is artificial. Where the two disagree, it is usually Hutcheson who is correct. The present case is no exception. It will be evident, on reflection, that there is something in breaking a promise which is bad in itself, quite independently of the consequences. Suppose someone who has promised to return your ten pounds lets you down. His letting you down usually hurts just as much as the loss of the ten pounds. Often it hurts far more. What hurts is the violation of your trust. This trust has a natural base. For example, a young child does not work out that his parents, on the whole, are not likely to deceive him and, on that basis, accepts what they say. He naturally accepts what they say. Indeed, in the beginning he accepts what everyone says. Much of this gets worn away as the years pass. But much of it persists. For example, if you are in a strange town and do not know your whereabouts, you will stop a passer-by, who is a complete stranger, and ask for directions. You never suppose that he will deliberately deceive you. This trust is valued in itself, being an aspect of the social instinct, which makes people crave the company of others. Many people, for example, would rather talk to anyone than not talk to anyone at all. This is not benevolence, any more than it is benevolence which leads the small child to trust those around him.

Now what makes promise-breaking so bad is that it exhibits the violation of trust in a flagrant form. When you ask a person to promise, you imply that you are prepared to extend your trust and therefore put it at stake. If that person now breaks your trust, he can do so only as a deliberate affront, for it has been specifically evoked. It is natural that this should arouse detestation, not simply when it occurs to you, but when you contemplate its occurring to others. This is the natural basis of promising. It is absurd to suppose that all this could arise simply from calculation. Indeed here, as so often, we find that utilitarian calculation is a later development which exploits material it cannot supply. Thus, once trust is lost, it cannot be restored by calculation. Only when it already exists can we work it to our advantage. It should be obvious, also, that there is no such contrast as Hume supposes between justice and our other duties. The duty of a parent arises because the care of children is something we naturally value. The duty to keep a promise arises because it exhibits that trust between people which we value as naturally as we do the care of children. The one is no more artificial than the other. Hume's fault is that he does not carry through his initial insight. Having criticized the social contract theorists for explaining society in utilitarian terms, he switches over, in the course of his account, precisely to those terms himself.

Kemp Smith argued that Hume's account of causality and of an independent world is derived from his account of morality. Whether or not Kemp Smith is correct about the chronological sequence, he is correct in implying that morality preeminently illustrates the theme of naturalism. Reason and will may develop or destroy value but they cannot create it. The sense of good and evil is thus irreducible to reason and will. It arises through the development of our nature as social beings. This development is itself a phenomenon of nature. At every stage in the development of a society there is more involved than its members have intended or can properly understand. Consequently it is no artificial creation but a natural growth, on which reason will depend. It follows that there can be no absolute distinction between what is a product of nature and what is a product of our own reason and will. For reason and will are themselves a product of nature. Here, preeminently, it is made apparent that our knowledge has its source in nature, not in ourselves.

8

REASON AND THEOLOGY

Hume's *Dialogues Concerning Natural Religion*, his main work in the philosophy of religion, is commonly held to be his most successful work. Indeed it is commonly held to have destroyed natural theology.[1] Natural theology assumes that the existence of God can be inferred from the existence of the world. It is held that Hume in the *Dialogues* shows this to be impossible by undermining the so-called argument from design. Now it is true that the *Dialogues* contains arguments which would have this effect, were they valid. In fact, as we shall see, they are fallacious. What is more to our present purpose, however, is that Hume never intended in the first place to destroy natural theology. The *Dialogues* itself affirms a version of the argument from design, not in passing, but at the climax of the work. In short, the work has been widely misrepresented. It has been eagerly received by numerous commentators who are sceptically inclined and has been interpreted in the light of their own scepticism. Thus they have assumed in its author motives he never entertained and conclusions he never attempted to prove. We must consider the matter in some detail.

It will be useful to begin by providing some background to the issues involved. We need, in particular, to consider the orthodox Christian view of the relation between reason and religious belief and then to consider how Hume stands in relation to that view. The view itself is perhaps most clearly developed by Calvin in the *Institutes*.[2] He holds that the existence of God is evident in his works. By the light of natural reasons, in other words, we may know from the existence of the world that God exists. But this is knowledge of a God who is transcendent. His ways are not our ways. Our knowledge, in short, is rather of his existence than of his nature. It is true that some knowledge of his nature is implicit in that of his existence. But that knowledge is negative or relative. For example, to say that God is omniscient is only to say that he is *not* limited in his wisdom. But what it is to be unlimited in wisdom is something of which we have no positive conception. To say that God is infinite is even more evidently to speak in the negative mode. For we are finite creatures and can have no conception, in direct terms, of any other existence. For Calvin, such negative knowledge cannot constitute a saving faith.

Indeed it may be worse than ignorance. For since God in his own nature is unknown, we are liable to construe him according to our ideas, to treat him in our image, which so far from saving us will lead us even further astray. As we shall see, Cleanthes in the *Dialogues* provides an excellent illustration of this point. Thus he denies that God is infinite, construes him rather as one empirical object amongst others, and treats him as differing from human beings not even in kind but simply in degree. For Calvin, a person is saved only through faith in what God has revealed, preeminently in Jesus Christ. When Paul was amongst the Greeks, he noted that they had an altar to an unknown God. He then proclaimed that this God had revealed himself through the prophets and, as their culmination, through the crucified and risen Christ. Calvin's view, likewise, is that through reasoning or proof one may arrive at the existence of an unknown God, but one can find salvation in this God only through faith in Christ and through the life of prayer and worship which is based on that faith.

The Catholic view of the relation between reason and religious belief is often assumed to differ sharply from the Protestant. Aquinas, in particular, is often treated as though he attempted to supply the Christian faith with a rational foundation.[3] The Protestant relies on faith, the Catholic – or so it is often assumed – attempts to support his faith with reason. But this view seems entirely mythical. On this issue, there seems no significant difference between Aquinas and Calvin. Thus Aquinas explicitly denies that faith requires the support of reason. There is nothing, he says, 'to stop someone accepting on faith some truth which that person cannot demonstrate, even if that truth in itself is such that demonstration could make it evident'.[4]

With regard to the transcendence of God, Aquinas expresses himself in terms which are as extreme as any found in Calvin. Brian Davies summarizes his view as follows.

> Aquinas does not mean us to believe that we have no knowledge of God. At the same time, however, he thinks that the nature of God is, in some sense, incomprehensible to us – that God defies our powers of understanding. People often say that God is mysterious, and Aquinas would agree. But the mystery of God is more radical for him than it is for many who proclaim it. As Herbert McCabe writes, in his view, 'When we speak of God, although we know how to use our words, there is an important sense in which we do not know what we mean....We know how to talk about God, not because of any understanding of God, but because of what we know about his creatures'.[5]

Aquinas, himself, expresses the point as follows: 'What is most strikingly certain is that the first cause surpasses human wit and speech. He knows God who owns that whatever he thinks and says falls short of what God really is.'[6]

It will be evident from the above passages that Aquinas's proofs of the existence of God – the so-called Five Ways – cannot be intended as a substitute for faith or as a ground from which faith follows simply as a consequence. Moreover, this is confirmed when we turn to the proofs themselves. What they seek to establish might be expressed by means of the following proposition from Aquinas: 'The principle of things is outside the world; so is its end.'[7]

In short, what they seek to establish about God does not go beyond what is contained in acknowledging his existence. Thus Aquinas is not seeking to base religious belief on reason alone. He is using reason to defend a faith which, for the most part, necessarily arises in other ways. There is no inconsistency in this procedure. Faith is different from reasoning but the two need not therefore be incompatible. The Christian has faith in a transcendent God who has revealed himself in Christ. But if the very idea of such a God is incoherent or in conflict with solid fact, the Christian faith is in vain. Aquinas's aim is not to ground faith on reason but to remove this obstacle. The Christian faith is not in this respect vain. Even someone who does not share the faith can appreciate that the idea of such a God is not incoherent and that there are reasons, independent of the faith, to believe in his existence. It is not *necessary* to faith that one appreciates those reasons. For someone may have a saving faith who has never considered them. It is not even *sufficient*. For someone who believes that the idea of God is incoherent may still not come to a saving faith even when he is disabused of that belief. The point is, however, that if he *continues* to hold that belief he will *certainly* not come to a saving faith. That obstacle at least will be removed.

In the view, therefore, both of the Catholic and the Reformed theology, faith takes precedence over reason. Newman, indeed, takes this as a mark of orthodoxy and treats the opposing view as heretical. The orthodox principle, he says:

> When brought out into words is as follows: that belief is in itself better than unbelief; that it is safer to believe; that we must begin with believing, and that conviction will follow; that as for the reasons of believing, they are for the most part implicit, and but slightly recognized by the mind that is under their influence; that they consist moreover rather of presumptions and guesses, ventures after the truth than of accurate proofs; and that probable arguments are sufficient for conclusions which we even embrace as most certain, and turn to the most important uses. *On the other hand, it has ever been the heretical principle to prefer Reason to Faith, and to hold that things must be considered true only so far as they are proved.*[my italics][8]

Now Newman's view was the one which tended to prevail amongst the vast majority of Christians, from the beginnings of Christianity until the seventeenth or eighteenth century. At that time, however, there occurred a change which we must consider in some detail, because it provides the context for Hume's *Dialogues*. During the eighteenth century it became a common view that faith or, as it was sometimes termed, enthusiasm, is inferior to reason, that it is, in any case, unnecessary to Christianity which is essentially reasonable, and that the truths of Christianity should therefore be established, like any other truth, on the basis of the evidence, or by rational demonstration. The spread of this view no doubt had various causes. But authorities on the period are agreed that one of the most important of these was the writings of John Locke.[9] That, also, is Hume's judgement.

> Locke seems to have been the first Christian, who ventured openly to assert, that *faith* was nothing but a species of *reason*, that religion was only a branch of philosophy, and that a chain of arguments, similar to that which established any truth in morals, politics or physics, was always employed in discovering all the principles of theology, natural and revealed.[10]

We need to pay special attention to this passage, for it gives us the theme of the *Dialogues*. It is Cleanthes who is speaking and he goes on to develop the view which he here attributes to Locke. It should be obvious that this view rests on a presupposition which is in conflict with Hume's own views. Cleanthes assumes that any truth in morals, politics or physics may be established by a chain of arguments or reasons. Hume has argued throughout the *Treatise* that in morals, politics and physics we rely ultimately on beliefs which do *not* rest on arguments or reasons. One of the main aims of the *Dialogues* is to show that the same is true of religion. In short, the aim of the work is not to attack religious belief as such, though Hume is of course critical of many of its manifestations. The work may be seen as continuing the argument of the *Treatise*. For its aim is to show that religion can rest on reason alone no more than morality or science.

But before considering the point in detail, we must return for a moment to Locke, so that we may have a better idea of the view which Hume was attacking. Hume's description of Locke's view is not altogether accurate. For example, Locke did not hold that a divine revelation can be established by argument or reason. According to Locke, where we are certain that a revelation is divine, we must accept what it says, even though we cannot prove it. What he held was that reason is required to show in the first place whether it is a divine revelation. At first sight, it is not entirely clear whether or not this is in conflict with what Newman calls the orthodox principle, namely, that faith takes precedence over reason. This becomes clearer, however, when we consider what Locke says elsewhere in his *Essay*. Newman quotes the following sentences.

How a man may know whether he be a lover of truth for truth's sake is worth inquiry; and I think there is one unerring mark of it, viz. the not entertaining any proposition with greater assurance, than the proofs it is built upon, will warrant....Enthusiasm fails of the evidence it pretends to; for men, thus possessed, boast of a light whereby, they say, they are enlightened, and brought into the knowledge of this or that truth. But if they know it to be a truth, they must know it to be so, either by its own self-evidence to natural reason, or by the rational proofs that make it out to be so.

Here Locke plainly argues that no one is entitled to hold a belief as true unless he can prove it by means of natural reason. In short, reason takes precedence over faith. Newman's comment is as follows.

Here this author lays down, that a lover of truth is he who loves a valid argument and that such faith as is not credulity or enthusiasm is always traceable to a process of reason, and varies with its cogency.

It will be worth quoting, also, Newman's own rejoinder to this view.

I will but observe on such philosophy as this, that, were it received, no great work ever would have been done for God's glory and the welfare of man. Enthusiasm may do much harm and act at times absurdly; but calculation never made a hero. [11]

Locke's view, in his own version or in some other, has been repeated innumerable times in the last two or three centuries as though it expressed an ultimate wisdom. But that only shows how easily we are all deceived by mere words, especially when they have a noble ring. For the view in fact is quite vacuous. As Locke is aware, it is incoherent to suppose that every belief must be supported by reason in the sense of some further belief which justifies it, for then we should be involved in an infinite regress. Every justification would itself need to be justified and so on ad infinitum. Some belief must be accepted in its own right, otherwise we shall never believe anything at all. Locke's view is that where a belief is accepted in its own right, that is because it is self-evident to our natural reason. But that is merely to equivocate in the use of 'reason'. Sometimes the term is used to signify some definite process, as when for example we sift through the evidence to determine whether a party is innocent or guilty. Sometimes it is a mere honorific label which we attach to any belief we feel entitled to hold. Locke sustains his view by an equivocation between the different usages, thereby creating the impression that every belief is or ought to be based on reason. But consider one of Hume's fundamental beliefs. We are all certain that there is an independent world. Therefore, according to Locke, we believe this because it is self-evident to our natural reason. But that is to cover over essential differences between the way we arrive at this belief and the way we arrive at others. Thus the way we arrive at the belief in an independent world bears no resemblance to the process of sifting evidence to determine whether a party is innocent or guilty. In the ordinary sense, people rarely reason about it at all. Moreover, where they do, as when for example they do philosophy, they do not find it self-evident to their reason. They find it involves various difficulties which they cannot immediately answer. Nevertheless, they remain quite certain it is true. But that is because, in the ordinary sense, it is obviously not based on reason at all.

We may note also in the passage from Locke that he already hints at a device so very frequently employed later in order to sustain his view. As he hints, people who rely on faith or enthusiasms have been led astray. The implication, at least for later rationalists, is that we cannot rely on it. But then, by a parallel argument, we cannot rely on reason. For there are occasions, literally innumerable, when people have been led astray who rely on reason.

In spite of its vacuity, however, Locke's view exerted an enormous influence. We may trace this influence in two different directions. The first influence is on Christianity itself. As we have noted, it became commonly accepted that Christianity could dispense with enthusiasm and rely simply on reason. There followed many attempts to give it a rational grounding, the most famous of these being found in the works of William Paley,[12] who gave a special place to the so-called argument from design. But rationalism within Christianity soon gave rise to a rationalism directed against it. This might have been foreseen. There is no easier way to introduce scepticism into a subject than to proceed on the principle that nothing shall be accepted until it is proved. The scepticism follows from the principle itself. That is because nothing can be proved by reason unless we are entitled to some beliefs we do not have to prove. Insist that you can prove everything you believe and you will soon find an opponent who points out that you are mistaken and then claims, on that ground, that you are not entitled to your beliefs. That is what happened to Christianity in the eighteenth century. Such names as Toland, Collins, Woolston and Chubb are now little known. But they were celebrities in their day. Taking the Christian apologists at their word, they adopted rationalism and produced a series of works which were still vaguely Deist but which had as their main object of attack Christianity itself.[13]

Our concern, however, is with rationalism as it appears in Christianity. Here we must pay special attention to the argument from design, for this was the argument on which the rationalists especially relied. At the start, however, it is quite essential to realize that this argument comes in different forms. We must distinguish, in particular, between the argument in its popular form, as it flourished in the eighteenth century, and in its classical form, as it appears for example in Aristotle or Aquinas, where it is sometimes called the teleological argument. In its popular form, it construes the order of the world by analogy with objects designed for human benefit and argues that as these objects need a designer, so the order of the world must have a designer analogous to the human.[14] The classical or teleological argument, by contrast, treats human design as a mere aspect of order in the world and argues that this order must have a source which transcends the world itself. In its classical form, it treats the order of the world as transcending the human order and God as transcending the order of the world. Thus in its first form, it tends to an anthropomorphic God; in its second, it leads to one who is transcendent.

The difference between the two forms has been well characterized by Ronald Knox. As he says, in its popular form the argument involves the assumption that you know what is best, and believe in God because you find him doing it.[15] Thus human beings need warmth and food. These are given through the sun above and the fields around us. Therefore God must exist in order to provide us with the sun and the fields. Here the order of the world is construed in terms of human benefit. The argument encounters difficulties with events such as an erupting volcano or an earthquake. For these do not work to human benefit. In fact an earthquake is no more an exception to the order of the world than is a field of wheat. The one may be explained as readily as the other in terms of natural law. The argument in its popular form is involved in this difficulty because it treats the whole order of the world as though it were designed for the purpose of human beings. By contrast, the argument in its classical form treats human beings as merely one element in an order which, in many of its aspects, transcends not simply human purpose but human understanding. As we shall see, this point is of quite vital significance to Hume in the *Dialogues*. He repeatedly stresses that what is at issue in the *Dialogues* is not the *existence* of God but his *nature*. He takes it as essential to the rationalist case that they can reveal, on purely rational ground, both the existence and the nature of God. The argument in its popular form answers to this purpose, for it seeks to establish the existence of a God who has the characteristics of a human father, who is good and loving, who has created a home for the sake of his children, and constantly tends and cares for them. The argument in its classical form answers to no such purpose. The order of the world is not designed for the sake of human beings and gives no immediate impression of goodness and love. It points to a source which is transcendent and therefore cannot be comprehended in human categories. As Aquinas said, the first cause surpasses wit and speech and he knows God who recognizes that he transcends all our knowledge.

As we have noted, the *Dialogues* has been a puzzle to many of its readers. Perhaps its most puzzling feature is that after spending the bulk of the work in criticizing the argument from design, Hume seems suddenly to turn around and defend the very same argument. This puzzlement will be eased when it is realized that the argument Hume defends is not the very same one he has been criticizing. In the bulk of the work, it is the argument in its popular form which Hume criticizes; what he defends, in the last section, is the argument in its classical form.

A purpose, an intention, a design strikes everywhere the most careless, the most stupid thinker, and no man can be so hardened in absurd systems, as at all times to reject it. *That nature does nothing in vain,* is a maxim established in all the schools, merely from the contemplation of the works of nature, without any religious purpose; and, from a firm conviction of its truth, an anatomist, who had observed a new organ or canal, would never be satisfied till he had also discovered its use and intention. One great foundation of the *Copernican* system is the maxim, *that nature acts by the simplest methods, and chooses the most proper means to any end;* and astronomers often, without thinking of it, lay this strong foundation of purity and religion. The same thing is observable in other parts of philosophy: And thus all the sciences almost lead us insensibly to acknowledge a first intelligent Author; and their authority is often so much the greater, as they do not directly profess that intention.[16]

Here Hume makes no attempt to liken the world to a product of human design. He points straight to the order of the world as it appears in scientific explanation. Science presupposes this order; it does not explain it. Nor does it explain itself. As Hume says elsewhere in the *Dialogues,* we may suppose as a theoretical possibility that the explanation lies in some self-sufficient principle inherent in the world itself. But such a principle is entirely unknown. In the nature of the case therefore we can have no direct evidence for its existence. Moreover, all the apparent evidence is against it. Nowhere do we experience the self-sufficient but only what presupposes something further. Again, as a theoretical possibility, we may suppose that the whole scheme consists of such contingencies stretching back to infinity. But that is to leave the scheme as a whole not simply unexplained but inexplicable. In the eighteenth century, such points as these were acknowledged and treated as decisive throughout the whole educated world. The existence of God was affirmed even by the most vociferous amongst the critics of Christianity. Voltaire is an obvious example. No doubt there were exceptions. It is said that when Hume was dining with d'Hollbach he remarked that he had never met an atheist. 'You have been unfortunate in your acquaintances,' said d'Hollbach, 'at the moment you are dining with seventeen.' The anecdote is perhaps apocryphal. But it is true to life in two respects. The first is that one would need to have been discriminating in the eighteenth century to have encountered any atheist, much less seventeen. The second is that the attitude it attributes to Hume is the one he really held. He did not believe that atheism was a serious issue.

That, of course, does not mean he was a Christian. His view seems to have been roughly the same as Voltaire's. This view is usually called deism. A deist may be likened to Calvin without his faith. In other words, like Calvin, he holds that natural reason has sufficient light to discern the existence of God but not to discern his nature. Unlike Calvin, he does not believe that this God has revealed himself in Jesus Christ. Let us note that this view is clearly distinguishable from agnosticism. The agnostic does not know whether or not there is a reality beyond this world. For all he knows, the world may be sufficient unto itself. By contrast, the deist is clear that the world does not explain itself. There is a reality beyond this world; but in the nature of the case it is incomprehensible to the human mind. Now that is roughly Philo's view in the *Dialogues*. His view is that the argument from design, so far as it is valid, cannot provide a rational foundation for Christianity, or any variety of popular religion, for it establishes no more than the existence of a God who in his own nature is unknown. The argument in its popular form goes further. But in that form, it is not valid.

It will be noted that Hume's quarrel is rather with persons of the type represented by Cleanthes than with Aquinas or Calvin. We may illustrate the point by referring to Philo's concluding words.

> A person, seasoned with a just sense of the imperfections of natural reason, will fly to revealed truth with the greatest avidity: While the haughty dogmatist, persuaded that he can erect a complete system of theology by the mere help of philosophy, disdains any further aid, and rejects this adventitious instructor. To be a philosophical sceptic is, in a man of letters, the most essential step towards being a sound, believing Christian; a proposition which I would willingly recommend to the attention of Pamphilus: And I hope Cleanthes will forgive me so far in interposing in the education and instruction of his pupil.[17]

Commentators treat this passage as ironic. In this they are correct. Unfortunately they often misunderstand where the irony lies. They take Hume to be implying that Christians are irrational because they cannot prove their fundamental beliefs and are forced to rely on faith. But that is an absurd interpretation, since it is in conflict with Hume's whole philosophy. On Hume's view, none of us can prove our fundamental beliefs.[18] Reason is impotent without belief to sustain it. It would be an evident inconsistency on his part to condemn the Christians simply for not proving theirs. The irony in Philo's remarks is that Hume himself does not share the faith they recommend. But from the point of view of those who do share that faith, what is said in the remarks he takes to be literally true. They are all ill-advised by those who, believing they can ground Christianity on reason alone, feel they can dispense with the aid of faith.

We find therefore that Hume's aim is not to eliminate but rather to limit the argument from design and in particular to show that it cannot provide a rational foundation for any variety of popular religion. His main aim is not to deny the rationality of religious beliefs as such, but to show that no form of religion can be grounded on reason alone. In this he is not even in conflict with orthodox Christianity which has always refused to give precedence to reason over faith. Hume does not share the Christian faith, but he would not, indeed he cannot, condemn it for refusing to give precedence to reason.

Inconsistencies

The above sketch of the background and main themes of the *Dialogues* has been drawn with firm lines. The lines may appear too firm, when we turn to the details of the work itself. For this, there are two reasons. The first is that Hume wished to write a genuine dialogue and therefore distributed sound points among its various protagonists, instead of confining them to one. Even Demea, for example, whom Hume is inclined to ridicule, makes a number of sound points in drawing attention to the unorthodox implications of Cleanthes' views. The second and more important reason lies in Hume's inconsistencies which are as apparent in the *Dialogues* as they are in the *Treatise*. We may illustrate this point by referring to the distinctions between the two forms of the argument from design. The distinction is implicit in what Hume says. But his empiricist assumptions make it impossible for him to draw it with any clarity.

The argument in its popular form rests on what we may term simple induction. There is a resemblance between objects of human design and objects in the natural world. Where A resembles B, we may assume that the cause of A resembles the cause of B. For example, if rain is falling outside, you will assume there are dark clouds in the sky, because there have been dark clouds in the sky whenever you have observed a similar phenomenon in the past. Consequently we may assume that objects of human design and natural objects have been caused by analogous processes of design. Stated in this form, the argument is very easily demolished. For example, present rain differs from past rain merely in degree. But objects of human design differ from natural objects in kind. Thus for most people the resemblances between the two are much less striking than the differences. This would suggest that their causes are not analogous.

As Hume makes clear in the *Dialogues*, there are many other objections. For example, the inference with regard to the clouds is based on a vast accumulation of experience. We have observed many instances of rain falling from clouds. We have observed, also, many instances of human objects being produced by design. But we have *never* experienced natural objects being so produced. Again, in the case of the clouds, we infer from one part of the world to another. But in the case of the argument from design, we infer from one part of the world to the whole. Out of the innumerable processes of nature, we select one, falling within our experience, to explain all the others. But the one falling within our experience occupies an infinitely small place within those we seek to explain. It is impossible to see therefore how it can sustain a valid induction. And so on.

Now Hume's own version of the argument at the end of the *Dialogues* does not depend on simple induction but presupposes that we have a sense of order which is not itself the product of experience. Thus he makes clear that a scientist, such as Copernicus, presupposes a principle of simplicity or of order in nature. There is no suggestion that he has arrived at this principle through noting a resemblance between natural objects and those of human design. Indeed there is a striking passage earlier in the dialogue where Cleanthes himself puts forward a version of the argument which is quite independent of simple induction.

> The declared profession of every reasonable sceptic is only to reject abstruse, remote and refined arguments; to adhere to common sense and the plain instincts of nature; and to assent, wherever any reasons strike him with so full a force, that he cannot, without the greatest violence, prevent it. Now the arguments for natural religion are plainly of this kind; and nothing but the most perverse, obstinate metaphysics can reject them. Consider, anatomize the eye: Survey its structure and contrivance; and tell me, from your own feeling, if the idea of a contriver does not immediately flow in upon you with a force like that of sensation.[19]

Here Cleanthes says that our sense of teleological structure is as *immediate* as any experience. But then it can hardly arise only as an *inference* from it. Moreover, it is obvious that Hume takes Cleanthes to have scored a hit, because he follows his speech with this passage: 'Here I could observe, Hermippus, that Philo was a little embarrassed and confounded: But while he hesitated in delivering an answer, luckily for him, Demea broke in upon the discourse, and saved his countenance.'[20]

Different versions of the argument from design are therefore present in the *Dialogues*. But the differences between them are never made explicit. The reason is that Hume shares many of the empiricist assumptions he attributes to Cleanthes. As we have seen, for example, he assumes that causal inference arises only through repeated experience. We can infer B from A only because the two have become associated in our minds through experiencing other instances of A and B. On this assumption, he can apparently account for a simple induction, such as the one about the dark clouds. But he cannot account for any other. In short, he cannot account for any inference about the facts which goes beyond simple induction. For that reason, he cannot clearly distinguish between different forms of the argument from design.

Now the *Dialogues*, as we have said, is widely held to have demolished natural theology. It has acquired this reputation through the arguments which Philo deploys, in the bulk of the work, against Cleanthes' version of the argument from design. It is therefore necessary to emphasize that the arguments both of Cleanthes and Philo rest on such assumptions as that a causal inference is equivalent to a simple induction or generalization from experience. In short, they rest almost exclusively on empiricist assumptions. These assumptions, were they valid, would certainly demolish natural theology. But then they would as readily demolish the whole of science. To see the point, let us consider one of the arguments. When we attribute design to the world as a whole, we attribute to the whole what we have experienced only in one of its parts. Our only experience of an object's being designed is confined to our experience of that process as it occurs amongst human beings, who occupy, whether in space or in time, only a minute portion of the world as a whole. The induction now seems invalid, for our experience seems insufficient to sustain so general a conclusion. Exactly the same point applies, however, to any general conclusion in science. The accumulated experience of all science covers, whether in space or in time, only a minute portion of the world as a whole. For example, a scientist assigns an absolute speed to light. Consider the light which has been shed throughout the history of the universe by the countless millions of stars. How much of this has been experienced by the scientist, or indeed by anyone else? Nevertheless the scientist assigns an absolute speed not simply to the light he has experienced but to all light throughout the entire history of the universe. It will be obvious on reflection that a scientist's experience would never lead him to a general conclusion unless he presupposes in nature a uniformity or order which he has not discovered through experience itself.

As we implied in an earlier chapter, scientific theory is based on hypothetical, not simple, induction. For example, Copernicus in developing his theory relied entirely on observations which were obtained by astronomers who held the Ptolemaic theory, the one opposed to his own. In short, the two opposing theories rest on the same body of observations. It is evident, therefore, that neither could have arisen as a simple generalization from those observations. The Copernican theory is preferred to the Ptolemaic not because it conforms to those observations, for so does the Ptolemaic, but because it provides for them the simpler or better explanation. The criterion is intellectual not empirical. The point is even more obvious in the case of the atomic theory. A solid object may be compressed. In short, it can be reduced in size without loss of matter. We assume that a solid object, below the phenomenal level, has gaps in it. This hypothesis is assumed for explanatory purposes, not because it follows from experience. It cannot follow from experience since we have never seen those gaps. There is an analogy, it is true, even on the phenomenal level between a solid object and one with gaps in it, for both may be compressed. On the phenomenal level, however, the resemblances between the two are considerably less striking than the differences. For example, to a physicist the gaps in a leaky boat differ only in degree from those in a sound one. On the phenomenal or empirical level, however, the difference is one of a kind, so that the differences between the two are far more striking than any resemblance. In short, the arguments which Philo employs in the *Dialogues* would as readily demolish the atomic theory as the argument from design.

We may note that Hume's empiricist assumptions show themselves not simply in the *Dialogues* but in his other writings on the philosophy of religion. There is a striking example in the *Enquiries*. He there seeks to establish the following conclusion.

> The religious hypothesis, therefore, must be considered only as a particular method of accounting for the visible phenomena of the universe; but no just reasoner will ever presume to infer from it any single fact, and alter or add to the phenomena, in any single particular.[21]

In other words, the hypothesis that God exists is in a manner useless, for it will not enable us to infer any fact about the world which we could not have obtained from considering the world itself. His argument for this is that the existence of God is inferred from the existence of the world as a cause from its effect. But in such an inference we are never entitled to attribute to the cause more than is needed to account for the effect. Therefore in inferring the existence of God from the existence of the world, we are not entitled to attribute to God more than is needed to account for the existence of the world. It is obvious, however, that this is not the conclusion Hume seeks to establish. He needs a further premise: in accounting for an effect by means of a cause, we need never attribute to the cause more than could already be found at the level of the effect. His conclusion now follows. Unfortunately, the premise we have added is plainly false. For example, in order to account for a phenomenon such as compression, we have to attribute properties to the cause which do not appear at all at the phenomenal level. In short, we cannot account for the effect unless we attribute to the cause properties which do *not* appear at the level of the effect. Hume falls into his fallacy because he assumes that we can never infer one event from another unless we have already experienced instances of both. It would then follow that we can never infer beyond what we have already experienced. But that assumption, as we have said, would undermine the whole of theoretical science.

We may go further. We have concentrated on showing that empiricist assumptions are inadequate to account for hypothetical induction or argument to the best explanation. We may thereby have given the impression that they are adequate to explain simpler forms of induction. But that is not so. Not even simple induction can be explained on purely empiricist assumptions. Indeed, if we consider it closely we shall find that it is merely a simplified version of an argument to the best explanation. Consider any simple empirical law, such as dark clouds produce rain, metal dissolves in acid, fire burns, etc. It is not through a mechanical accumulation of observations that even these laws arise; rather they are instinctively adopted as the best explanation for those observations. Suppose whenever you visit a person, at whatever time of day, you find him drunk. You do not assume he just happens to be drunk whenever you visit him. You assume he is always or usually so. For that provides the best explanation for why, whenever you visit him, you find him drunk. Now out of all the fire which has occurred in the history of the world we have observed only a random sample. In this respect, our observations are analogous to the random visits you pay your neighbour. In a similar way, we do not assume that fire just happens to burn only when we see or feel it. We assume it always does. For that provides the best explanation for why, whenever we see or feel it, we find it burns.

Observations, however numerous, are random with regard to the operations of nature. For these operations continue in the same way whether or not we observe them. Consequently observation in itself could never give rise to the idea of law. It is not the observations which explain the law but the law which explains the observations. We can use observation to select the laws which in fact operate only because we already have an instinctive grasp of nature as law-like or orderly. Thus unless we already had the idea of law, we should never arrive at it through sense experience. It is only Hume's empiricist assumptions which prevent his clearly grasping this point, since it follows from his own analysis of causality. As he shows, it is not through mere experience of the objective process that we arrive at the idea of cause. We arrive at it because we are already predisposed to treat our experience in causal terms.

We may go further still. Empiricist assumptions are even less adequate to explain our grasp of design or intention. Early in the *Dialogues*, Philo argues as follows.

> If we see a house, Cleanthes, we conclude, with the greatest certainty, that it had an architect or builder; because this is precisely that species of effect, which we have experienced to proceed from that species of cause.[22]

In short, you cannot infer an effect from an intention or a design unless you have experienced the intention or design producing that effect. The conclusion seems easily to follow. Since you have never experienced God's designing the world, you cannot infer from the world that it was designed by God. Now as Reid pointed out, what Hume here assumes is almost the reverse of the truth. It would be nearer the truth to say that one cannot experience intention or design unless one can infer it from its effects. For it is only through its manifestations that we can ever experience intention or design. To see this point, let us consider Hume's example. You take a house to have been produced by intention or design because you have experienced the intention or design producing the house. But what precisely does this mean? You may have seen the operations of the builder and his workmen and later you may see the house emerge. But in saying that the house is produced by design, you presuppose the movements of the workmen are intentional, having the house as their end. But in what sense do you see this? It cannot be in the sense that you see the workmen's movements, because when you see their movements the end does not exist. You take their movements to have this intention but that is not because you see the intention producing those movements. You have nothing but the movements to go on. In short, it is only through its manifestations that you can ever experience intention or design. Unless you already take the movements as intentional, you cannot experience them as intentional at all. As Reid pointed out, Hume's argument leads inevitably to solipsism. The same argument which makes it impossible for us to grasp God's design as manifested in the world would make it equally impossible for us to grasp our neighbour's design as manifested in his words or actions.

It is evident that our grasp of design is no more the product of experience than is our grasp of causality. Certainly through experience you may change your mind and attribute to an action this intention rather than that one. But then you already have a grasp of intention. What is absurd is to suppose that your very grasp of this notion might have been inferred from some prior set of experiences not involving such a grasp. The very process of inference is intentional. Our grasp of causality and of intention are merely different aspects of that sense of order without which we should be incapable of intelligible experience.

Now it is this order which is the starting point for the argument from design in its classical form. It argues that the order of the world cannot be explained by reference to any feature of the world which does not presuppose it. This applies even to the simplest empirical law. Thus the law that fire burns is not reducible to any set of empirical instances. It applies as much to the fires we have never experienced as to those we have, and as much to those that will exist or to those that have existed already. It is therefore irreducible to any set of empirical features. Consequently the source of order cannot lie within the world but only in what transcends it. It is natural that we should speak of this source as mind or person. That is not because we have noted a resemblance between the divine mind and our own, which is absurd. It is because mind represents for us order in its most complex or developed form. Consequently we cannot conceive of order as having its source in what lies below the level of mind. In speaking of God as mind we therefore speak in a sense figuratively, but not falsely.

As we have implied, the inconsistencies in the *Dialogues* are parallel to those in the *Treatise*. In the *Treatise*, Hume's criticism of rationalism is threatened at a number of points by complete scepticism, this arising from his empiricist assumptions. Similarly, in the *Dialogues*, the empiricist assumptions which are involved in the bulk of the work lead Hume towards a conclusion more sceptical than he either desires or intends. He attempts to counteract this tendency in the last section of the work. Philo there states and affirms a version of the argument from design which is clearer and more forceful than

113

any in the bulk of the work. But perhaps the most significant passage is the one in which Cleanthes supports Philo by referring in the following terms to what he calls the religious theory or hypothesis.

> Whoever attempts to weaken this theory, cannot pretend to succeed by establishing in its place any other that is precise and determinate: it is sufficient for him, if he starts doubts and difficulties; and by remote and abstract views of things, reach that suspense of judgement, which is here the utmost boundary of his wishes. But besides that this state of mind is in itself unsatisfactory, it can never be steadily maintained against such striking appearances as continually engage us into the religious hypothesis. A false, absurd system, human nature, from force of prejudice is capable of adhering to with obstinacy and perseverance: But no system at all, in opposition to a theory, supported by strong and obvious reason, by natural propensity, and by early education, I think it absolutely impossible to maintain or defend.[23]

Here, as in the *Treatise*, Hume responds to scepticism by switching from empiricism to naturalism. Where a person has no system of his own, he may raise objections, even unanswerable ones, to the prevailing system. But these objections will usually be futile, because they do not have behind them a system, like the prevailing one, which is based not simply on a show of reason but on natural propensity and common opinion. In the modern age, at least in the industrialized countries of the West, there are many who find in atheism a system which satisfies both intellect and feeling. To Hume and his contemporaries, this attitude was inconceivable. Hume takes for granted that the religious system has behind it common feeling and natural propensity. For him, of course, natural propensity has *epistemological* and not just emotive significance. In the absence of overwhelming objections, one is *entitled* to hold to those beliefs which natural propensities support. Now in Hume's day there was no alternative system to the religious, similarly precise and determinate and similarly backed by natural propensity. The religious theory was, as it were, the only one in the field. As Cleanthes says, reasoning of the sceptical or atheistic type could aspire to no more than suspense of judgement. But, as he also says, suspense of judgement can never prevail against reasons which have behind them common feeling and natural propensity. That is why Hume believes that complete freedom of discussion on the more abstruse topics of religion is safer than on any other topic.

> I must confess [says Philo] that I am less cautious on the subject of natural religion than on any other; both because I know that I can never on that hand, corrupt the principles of any man of common

sense, and because no one, I am confident, in whose eyes I appear a man of common sense, will ever mistake my intention.[24]

Free discussion could not do harm because there was no alternative to the religious system. Atheism was not a live issue. To see these points more clearly, let us turn to the details of the work itself.

The *Dialogues*

The *Dialogues*, as we have noted, is a work which puzzles many of its readers. It will be useful if we begin with four points which, if they are borne in mind, will make it easier to grasp the structure of the work.

First, Hume does *not* hold that the argument from design is simply fallacious or invalid. On the contrary, he acknowledges its force. When he contemplates the order of the world, he too is led to treat it as the manifestation of what transcends the world. As we shall see, there are a number of points in the *Dialogues* where Hume indicates this, even before Philo affirms a version of the argument in the last section.

Second, although he acknowledges the force of the argument, he is puzzled to explain where its force lies. As we have seen, this is because of his empiricist assumptions. He holds that I can infer B from A only where the two have become associated in my mind. They become thus associated because I have repeatedly experienced instances which are exactly like them. The instances must be exactly like them, or almost exactly so, for otherwise they cannot give rise to an association which is automatic or mechanical. But it is only where the association is automatic or mechanical that I am forced, on seeing A, to infer B. In short, the certainty of the inference depends on its being produced mechanically by the repetition of exactly similar instances. Hume's problem is now obvious. When we infer the existence of God from our experience of the world, we make an inference which passes beyond our sensory experience. But in his view, it is only within sensory experience that we can be certain of any inference. We can infer B from A only where we have experienced instances of both. We may note that this, for Hume, is a recurrent problem. For example, he has an exactly parallel problem in accounting for our knowledge of an independent world. In his view, we can know the physical world only through sensory experience, but the physical world is independent of that experience and therefore transcends it. Consequently, in order to know an independent world, we should have to move from our sensory experience to a belief which transcends that experience. The trouble is that on his empiricist assumptions that move is impossible.

Third, this, nevertheless, does not make him deny the force of the inference from the world to God. He does not deny this, any more than he denies the belief in an independent world. What he insists, however, is that when one infers from the world to God, one is making an inference which in some manner *transcends* experience. The inference is not in the ordinary sense empirical, as when one infers one empirical object from another. Consequently, the God to whom one infers must himself be *transcendent*. He is not one empirical object amongst others, whose nature can be explained in ordinary terms. But that, in effect, is precisely the view which is held by Cleanthes. He holds that the argument from design is an ordinary empirical argument which, in establishing the existence of God, reveals also his nature as analogous to our own, as differing from ours only in degree. The bulk of the *Dialogues* has as its aim to undermine precisely that view. As we shall see, Hume's arguments are very variable in quality. Some of them rest on empiricist assumptions which are so crude that Cleanthes might have rebutted them simply by referring to the practices of eighteenth-century science. But others are of great power, the most successful being those in Parts X and XI, where Philo asks Cleanthes to reconcile the order of the world with any scheme of morality comprehensible to the human mind.

Fourth, since, in the bulk of the work, Philo has been concerned with the argument from design in the form presented by Cleanthes, he does *not* contradict himself when in the last section he himself affirms a version of that argument. The God whom he affirms transcends human reason, being in his nature incomprehensible to us. The God whom Cleanthes affirms is anthropomorphic. It is the God, Hume believes, of popular religion. As the concluding pages make clear, popular religion has been throughout an object of attack. Hume believes it to be pernicious in all its effects. It is because popular religion draws support from the argument in Cleanthes' form that he has been concerned to demolish it. This does not prevent his affirming the argument in his own form, for in that form it gives no support to popular religion.

With these points in mind we may now turn to the *Dialogues*. Parts I and II are concerned to set the topic for debate and to display the opposing views of Philo and Cleanthes. The work begins with a distinction between natural theology, taken as a science or study, and the practice of religion itself. Demea remarks that in any scheme of education the child should be instructed from the beginning in the principles of religion. But natural theology, the science or study of religion, should be reserved for the later stages of his education, when his mind has matured and he has already been instructed in the other branches of philosophy. Philo commends this scheme. It has the advantage of discouraging pride and self-sufficiency. Those who come too early to the study of natural theology will possess only a little philosophy and will have acquired an exaggerated sense of what human reason can achieve. The cure for this is what Demea recommends, a more thorough preparation in philosophy, which will reveal the limits of human reason. The student who is well prepared in philosophy will know that the obscurities and perplexities which abound in natural theology are not peculiar to religion but are common to all branches of learning. Indeed, they arise when we reflect even on the humblest matters.

> When the coherence of the parts of a stone, or even that composition of parts, which renders it extended; when these familiar objects, I say, are so inexplicable, and certain circumstances so repugnant and contradictory; with what assurance can we decide concerning the origin of the world, or trace their history from eternity to eternity?[25]

Cleanthes now enters the discussion. He is disinclined to take Philo seriously. He takes him to be espousing a form of extreme or Pyrrhonian scepticism. Such scepticism is refuted by the behaviour of those who espouse it. In their philosophy they pretend that all is doubtful. But in everyday affairs they reason and act with the same certainty as everyone else.

In fact Philo is not espousing extreme scepticism and he is serious in his views. Indeed his views are identical with those which Hume has expressed in the *Treatise* and the *Enquiries*. What he advocates is mitigated not extreme scepticism. We are under a necessity to reason and to act. That is not denied. The effect of philosophy is not to undermine reason but to curb its pretensions. Thus a person who is familiar with perplexities of philosophy will continue to acknowledge the usefulness of reason. But he will be aware also of its delusions, and he will be quick to detect when it seeks to pass beyond its legitimate sphere. As we shall see, Philo will allow that reason may affirm the existence of God. What he denies, however, is that it is thereby equipped to explain his nature. We cannot explain the nature of ordinary matter, though we know it exists. How much less likely are we to explain the source of all being.

But Cleanthes now lays down his challenge. He will show that one may demonstrate, by a simple extension of ordinary reasoning, both the existence and the nature of God. His argument is as follows.

> The curious adapting of means to ends, throughout all nature, resembles exactly, though it much exceeds, the productions of human contrivance; of human design, thought, wisdom, and intelligence. Since therefore the effects resemble each other, we are led to infer, by all the rules of analogy, that the causes also resemble; and that the Author of nature is somewhat similar to the mind of man; though possessed of much larger faculties, proportioned to the grandeur of the work, which he has executed. By this argument *a posteriori*, and by this argument alone, do we prove at once the existence of a Deity, and his similarity to human mind and intelligence.[26]

Philo responds with two points of criticism. The first is that the inference from B to A is certain only where we have already experienced exactly similar instances. We have never experienced God's creating exactly similar worlds.

We have experience only of this one. Moreover, we have never seen God creating it. Second, Cleanthes is forced to rely on an analogy between part and whole. The whole universe with its innumerable processes is treated by analogy with one of its processes, namely, human design. But in the nature of the case a whole cannot be exactly similar to one of its parts. The analogy, in short, is bound to be a weak one. Amongst the numerous processes of nature, human design occupies a very small part. Why pick on this part to explain the whole? A great deal of the *Dialogues* is occupied in elaborating the consequences of these points. What are we to make of them? They have a certain force when taken ad hominem. For they are based on the type of reasoning to which Cleanthes commits himself. He argues, for example, that the processes of nature *exactly resemble*, though they much exceed, the productions of human contrivance. But the reader may wonder whether he might not have committed himself to a somewhat subtler form of reasoning.

The point is immediately apparent in Cleanthes' rejoinder. According to Philo, we cannot infer from the world to God, since there is only a single world and we have never seen God create it. But there is only a single earth and we have never seen it move. Nevertheless, Philo does not scruple to accept the Copernican theory. Cleanthes might have added that Galileo supported the Copernican theory by an analogy between whole and part. For example, he pointed out that when the shore is out of sight, we cease to detect the motion of our boat. He then argued by analogy that the motion of the earth would similarly be undetected. Here the condition of the whole is treated by analogy with one of its parts. In short, Philo's criticism seems to dispose as readily of the Copernican theory as of Cleanthes' argument.

Philo rejects this view. He denies that there is a single earth. There are many earths, for there is a clear analogy between our earth and the other planets. Cleanthes replies, correctly, that this was the very point at issue. On the Ptolemaic theory, there was no such analogy, for the planets were in motion whilst the earth was at rest. In short, the analogy between the earth and the planets is likely to be apparent only to someone who *already* accepts the Copernican theory. Cleanthes' main point can be illustrated as easily by reference to other theories in modern science. We may take as an instance the theory of evolution. This offers an explanation for the development of all the species on earth. But it is not supported by experience of exactly similar species on exactly similar planets. We know of no such species. In short, we are dealing with what, so far as our experience goes, is a unique case. Consequently scientists can arrive at a theory which covers the whole only by extrapolating from their experience of a part. But the part that scientists can experience is minute. We are dealing with a process which covers many millions of years and involves details so multitudinous that they cannot be adequately imagined, much less experienced. Thus the theory is not supported by the experience of exactly similar cases, nor has the process it postulates ever been observed. Moreover, scientists arrive at the theory by

118

extrapolating from a part, indeed a minute part, to a whole. Were we to accept Philo's criticisms, we should have difficulty in explaining why the theory has ever been taken seriously. Nevertheless, many people in our own day would treat the theory as a paradigm of scientific reasoning. In short, we already have cause to suppose that Philo's criticisms rest on an oversimplified idea of what it is to reason about matters of fact. In Part II Cleanthes resumes his defence. He offers an analogy: 'Suppose that there is a natural, universal, invariable language, common to every individual of the human race; and that books are natural productions, which perpetuate themselves in the same manner with animals and vegetables, by descent and propagation.'[27]

Kemp Smith finds this example perplexing and takes it 'to illustrate Cleanthes' entire failure to recognize the point and force of Philo's criticisms'.[28] In fact, Cleanthes' point seems clear. Philo has ruled out any real analogy between the natural and the human order, *however great the resemblance between the two*. To illustrate the point, Cleanthes imagines a resemblance between natural objects, plants, and human objects, books, which is so great that one may read the one as easily as the other. Imagine, in short, that natural objects actually communicated with us. For Philo, this would still give us little or no reason to discern any manifestation of intelligence in the natural order. That is because we have *seen* intelligence producing books but have never *seen* intelligence producing objects in the natural order. Cleanthes' implication is that Philo is simply refusing on a priori grounds to acknowledge any real analogy between the natural and the human order.

We must add that Kemp Smith repeatedly exaggerates the force of Philo's initial criticisms. For example, he takes it as a *decisive* objection to Cleanthes' argument that order is 'internal' to natural objects but is imposed 'externally' on machines. What he means is that machines are constructed by creatures which are not machines whereas natural objects such as trees and flowers arise out of other trees and flowers. Indeed he has a complicated theory according to which Hume moved from deism to atheism, or what is virtually atheism, simply through recognizing the implications of this point. But the objection to which he refers, so far from being decisive, is no real objection at all. For we can easily imagine an order which is in that sense internal holding amongst machines. Thus we can imagine machines which assemble machines which assemble further machines and so on indefinitely, so that, after a time, people will never have seen machines produced in any other way. Nevertheless, they would be correct in inferring that a sufficient explanation for this order must involve referring at some point to something other than machines. In short, it is irrelevant that the order is 'internal'. The point is that it is not *self-explanatory*. But the order which holds among trees and flowers is no more self-explanatory than the one we have imagined holding amongst machines. Cleanthes' point, in effect, is that if we should expect an explanation in one case why not in the other. It is clear that the objection to which Kemp Smith refers has no bearing at all on the point.[29]

Cleanthes now restates his argument, expressing it on this occasion with considerable force.

> The declared profession of every reasonable sceptic is only to reject abstruse, remote and refined arguments; to adhere to common sense and the plain instincts of nature; and to assent, wherever any reasons strike him with so full force, that he cannot, without the greatest violence, prevent it. Now the arguments for natural religion are plainly of this kind; and nothing but the most perverse, obstinate metaphysics can reject them. Consider, anatomize the eye: Survey its structure and contrivance; and tell me, from your own feeling, if the idea of a contriver does not immediately flow in upon you with a force like that of a sensation. The most obvious conclusion surely is in favour of design; and it requires time, reflection and study, to summon up those frivolous, though abstruse, objections, which can support infidelity....
>
> Some beauties in writing we may meet with, which seem contrary to rules, and which gain the affections, and animate the imagination, in opposition to all the precepts of criticism, and to the authority of the established masters of art. And if the argument for theism be, as you pretend, contradictory of the principles of logic; its universal, its irresistible influence proves clearly, that there may be arguments of a like irregular nature. Whatever cavils may be urged; an orderly world, as well as a coherent articulate speech, will still be received as an incontestable proof of design and intention.
>
> It sometimes happens, I own, that the religious arguments have not their due influence on an ignorant savage and barbarian, not because they are obscure and difficult, but because he never asks himself any question with regard to them. Whence arises the curious structure of an animal? From the copulation of its parents. And these whence? From *their* parents. A few removes set the objects at such a distance, that to him they are lost in darkness and confusion; nor is he actuated by any curiosity to trace them farther. But this is neither dogmatism nor scepticism, but stupidity; a state of mind very different from your sifting inquisitive disposition, my ingenious friend.[30]

Philo is now in considerable difficulty. The essence of his mitigated scepticism is that one should accept reason or belief where it has a natural force, whatever the difficulties of explaining it on philosophical ground. There is no doubt that he feels the force of the argument, as Cleanthes now states it, and he has nothing to set against it but philosophical speculation. Hume signals the point by drawing our attention to Philo's embarrassment. Later, it will transpire that Philo is prepared to acknowledge the argument in this form.

But for him to have acknowledged it at this point would have been to bring the dialogue to a premature close. Consequently Hume introduces Demea to turn the course of the conversation.

Part IV opens with Demea elaborating his theme. He is concerned with the unorthodox implications of Cleanthes' views. If the existence of God is to be proved by empirical analogy, there must be a similarity between the divine and the human mind which can be described in empirical terms. But is it not essential to orthodox belief that God transcends the empirical? To the divine mind we attribute infinity, perfect immutability and simplicity. Where are the empirical analogues for these qualities? Cleanthes responds to this criticism by rejecting the attributes. He will not allow that the divine mind is infinite, simple and immutable.

> A mind, whose acts and sentiments and ideas are not distinct and successive; one, that is wholly simple and totally immutable; is a mind which has no thought, no reason, no will, no sentiment, no love, no hatred; or in a word is no mind at all.[31]

He has now delivered himself into Philo's hands. For he has committed himself to the view of God as differing from the human only in degree. Philo begins by pointing out that whilst we explain events by referring to mental operations we also explain mental operations by referring to further events. Consequently we are as entitled to ask for an explanation of order in the divine mind as to ask for an explanation of order in the world. If the divine mind explains the world, what explains the divine mind? The dilemma seems acute. If the divine mind itself is to be explained by further causes then, in any traditional sense, it hardly seems divine. On the other hand, if it requires no explanation, its difference from the human is radical, not one of degree.

But here Philo overplays his hand. He argues further that if the divine mind, as much as the world, needs explanation, there is no point in explaining the world by reference to the divine mind. One might as well remain on the level of the world. That might be termed the Cartesian fallacy. As we have seen, the Cartesians objected to Newton's explaining the relations between the planets by means of gravitational attractions. Their objection was that since Newton could not explain gravitational attraction, he was not entitled to refer to it in explaining the relations between the planets. Newton replied, in effect, that the condition of explaining an event A is that we can specify an event B which explains it. The condition is *not* that we can in addition explain event B. Cleanthes replies to Philo in similar terms. Philo says that Cleanthes would be correct, were they dealing with *general* causes. But in fact they are dealing with the *particular* cause of a *particular* effect. The reply is weak, since Cleanthes has already denied the validity of the distinction.

Part V reveals, however, that Cleanthes' respite is temporary. The premise of his argument is that there is some resemblance or analogy between a part of the world and the world as a whole which will enable us to infer that the cause of the world as a whole is analogous to the cause of that part. Philo proceeds to argue that this premise will yield a variety of hypotheses each as plausible as Cleanthes' own. The argument is extended, covering Part V through to Part VIII. In Part V, Philo accepts the assumption that the world is analogous to the productions of the human mind. Still, why assume that it is the production of a single mind? Most human production is co-operative. Indeed, even the craftsman who works alone has inherited his skills from other craftsmen. Why then not accept polytheism? Perhaps the world has been produced by a team of gods. In Part VI, Philo considers whether we should not take our analogy from the human body rather than from the human mind. Perhaps the world is one great body and what we call God is really its soul. In Part VII, he points out that vegetative order is more extensive than human order. Why should we not suppose that the world has been generated in the manner of a vegetable? In Part VIII he considers why we should suppose order to be fundamental. Perhaps it has arisen through chance out of an original chaos. None of these hypotheses, he acknowledges, is very plausible in itself. His point is that each is as plausible or as implausible as the one offered by Cleanthes.

Philo's arguments, however, are somewhat wearisome in their details. The reason is that they have a certain force ad hominem, but otherwise no force at all. They will seem impressive only to someone who identifies all reasoning about the facts with the simplest type of empirical inference. It will be useful to deal with the point in some detail.

As we have seen, Hume assumes that an inference from B to A arises through repeated experience of similar instances. He has a comparable view of analogy. On his view, an analogy between two objects is pressed on us by the overwhelming number of resemblances between the two. This means that there can be no analogy between the human order and the order of the world unless the quantity of similarities between them vastly outweighs the quantity of differences. It means, also, that if the vegetative order is more extensive than the human, the order of the world is bound to bear less analogy to the human order than to the vegetative. Or again, if there is an analogy between the natural order and human production and if human production is *more often* joint than individual, the *greater* analogy must be with joint production. But this is a radically defective view of analogy. An analogy is a point of resemblance between objects which otherwise may be quite *unlike*. When the poet compares his love to a red, red rose, he is not suggesting that the two are virtually indistinguishable. Moreover, analogy is purposive not mechanical. Thus a person who makes an analogy is not seeking to register a quantitative similarity; he is drawing our attention to a resemblance which he takes to be significant. For example, in pointing to a resemblance between objects which otherwise are quite unalike, he may be seeking to reveal aspects of those objects we should not have seen for ourselves. Similarly, it is not in order to register a quantitative similarity that someone makes an analogy between the human and the natural order; his aim is to draw our attention to a resemblance which he takes to be significant. Until we know what he takes to be significant, we are in no position to assess his analogy.

The above points apply as readily to the use of analogy in science. No more in science than anywhere else do analogies arise simply from the pressure of quantitative similarity. They are introduced because they have a significance, and they derive their significance from the attempt to raise or to resolve some *problem*. We may illustrate this by reference to the atomic theory. The theory may be said to arise from certain resemblances between solid and non-solid objects. For example, both may be compressed. But many have noticed this resemblance without its giving rise in their minds to a theory. Plainly a theory will not arise until someone ceases to take the resemblance for granted and finds in it a puzzle or problem. How is it to be accounted for? We can account for compression in a non-solid body. It is caused by the gaps in it. May we not therefore infer by analogy that there are gaps in the solid body? But obviously on the empirical level a solid body does *not* have gaps in it. The empirical differences between a solid and a non-solid body outweigh the similarities. We have now exhausted reasoning about the facts as Philo and Cleanthes conceive of it. Unfortunately we have not yet arrived at the atomic theory. To arrive at this, we have to suppose that solid objects have a structure which does not appear at all at the empirical level. How is that supposition to be justified? Plainly it cannot be justified simply by an inference from empirical resemblances. It cannot be justified at all unless one feels the problem that compression raises. But then it may be justified as the only or best way of solving that problem. In short, the atomic theory is justified by its *explanatory force*; it is not forced on us by empirical resemblances. The criterion is intellectual not empirical. We now have a conception of reasoning about the facts altogether different from the one suggested by Philo and Cleanthes. We are no longer seeking to explain the world simply by an inference from empirical sequences. We are seeking to discover the intelligible order which underlies those sequences.

Let us take the point further. How are we to conceive of the structure which we are now attributing to solid objects? It is atomic. But what is an atom? Is it just like an empirical object but very much smaller? We must consider whether that question does not rest on a false supposition. If an atom were just like an empirical object, it would be an object on the empirical level. But the point is that we have left that level. Precisely what we have discovered is that the empirical level, beyond a certain point, is inadequate for understanding physical reality. But then if we use an empirical model to describe the atom, it must be symbolic rather than literal, justified by the consequences of its use rather than by its being, in the empirical sense, a literal picture of what is being described. The point has become the more evident the more science has developed. For example, people were inclined at first to treat the atom in empirical terms. They treated it as though it were like a very tiny billiard ball. It has long been evident that the error in this is radical. It is not that the atom is less like a billiard ball than some other empirical object. The error is in supposing that there is some empirical object which in that sense the atom is like. It consists in a failure to grasp that physical reality transcends the empirical and therefore that beyond a certain point it cannot be understood in empirical terms. This error is no longer so easy to make. For in contemporary science the models commonly used are not even coherent when taken on the empirical level. For example, a fundamental constituent of matter may be taken both as a particle and as a wave. We can treat an empirical object either as a wave or as a particle but we cannot treat it as both without supposing that in the meantime it has changed its nature. The same point arises when the scientific concept of a wave is applied to light. A wave in empirical terms is the shape of some substance. Thus a sea wave is a certain shape taken by the sea water. At first a light wave was treated in somewhat similar terms and a substance – the ether – was posited as its medium. At the turn of the century the ether was abandoned. But scientists still speak of light waves, leaving us with a wave that is, as it were, bodiless and answers to no empirical reality. At this point it becomes obvious that scientists have long since abandoned the attempt to understand physical reality in terms of empirical similarities.

Now in the light of these points, let us consider how Cleanthes, were he living today, might reconstitute his argument. He would draw an analogy between the natural and the human spheres; but that is obviously not because the two are so overwhelmingly alike. At first sight the differences outweigh the similarities, as they do between solid and non-solid objects. He is drawing attention to a point of resemblance, the order which holds in the two spheres. But this in itself gets us nowhere, so long as it is simply taken for granted. We need to find it puzzling. How is it to be accounted for? For example, does science, in explaining the natural world, also explain its order? He would argue, as indeed Hume later argues, that it does not do so. Science always presupposes order in the world; it does not explain it. He would then argue that a shift is needed here, comparable in some respects with the shift involved in the atomic theory. We must see the order of the world as a manifestation of what transcends the world, as we may come to see the empirical phenomenon of compression as revealing a structure which transcends the empirical. In this, he would be assisted by an inference which is natural or instinctive to the mind. As Reid pointed out, it is natural for us to treat order as a manifestation of what transcends it. In the human sphere, for example, we do not experience behaviour as distinct from mind and then search for a link between the two. We immediately treat behaviour as intentional and therefore as a manifestation of mind. A similar point is evident in Part III of the *Dialogues*, where Cleanthes expresses his argument in a different and more powerful form. As he implies, when we contemplate the order of the world, as distinct from simply taking it for granted, we treat it, by an instinctive or immediate inference, as having an intentional source. It is natural also that we should treat this source as akin to mind. That is because it is only in mind that we find an image for the source of order. To see this, consider Philo's comparison between the human and the vegetative order. He argues that the vegetative is more extensive than the human and therefore that we have no reason to treat mind as the more fundamental. The question, however, is not which is more extensive but which has the more *explanatory force*. And it is evident that we should give the preference to mind, for mind is not simply ordered; it is *aware* of order both in other things and in itself. The acorn, as it grows into an oak, exhibits order. But we do not think of it as the source of the order it exhibits. A human being, in creating a poem, exhibits order but is also in some measure its source, for it is through his awareness of its order that the poem exists. Here, in mind, we have an image for the source of order. But are we then supposing that the divine mind is strictly analogous to the human? The question is meaningless. We might as well ask whether a light wave is really like a wave in the sea. In both cases, we are dealing with a model or image not with an analogy based on empirical similarities. For the reality in each case transcends us and we are forced to make of it what sense we can, in the only terms available to us. God, being transcendent, can be described only in terms which are appropriate to our own condition, not to his.

Here Cleanthes' argument is no longer an empirical inference; it is reconstituted as an argument to the best explanation. In this form, the transcendence of God is preserved; he is not one empirical object amongst others. But we must add immediately that our Cleanthes is no longer Hume's. Moreover, his Cleanthes was not a mere figment of his imagination but was intended to represent real figures who did argue for a God in the empirical or anthropomorphic mode. We must continue, therefore, with Hume's treatment.

Part IX provides an interlude. Demea suggests that Cleanthes is mistaken in attempting to prove the existence of God by an argument in the a posteriori form. In its place, he offers an a priori argument. Whatever comes into existence has a cause which itself has a cause which yet again has its cause, and so on indefinitely. Here we have a chain of events, each of which is explained by some further event. But how are we to explain the existence of the whole chain? It must have its source in what does not come into existence but exists necessarily and will explain both itself and the chain as a whole.

Cleanthes rejects this reasoning as fallacious. He offers two criticisms. One is that Demea commits the fallacy of composition. If we explain each link in a chain, we do not need an explanation for the chain as a whole. We have already explained that, in explaining the individual links. But this criticism is itself fallacious. It presupposes that in the chain of events which Demea describes each event has been given a *sufficient* explanation. But that, in effect, is precisely what Demea denies. Suppose we explain the existence of A by reference to B. If B is contingent, we have as yet no explanation for its existence. But then we cannot have a *sufficient* explanation for the existence of A. For A depends on B for its existence. Moreover, the point remains the same however we extend the chain, so long as the explanations involved are contingent. Suppose we explain the existence of B by reference to C. If C is contingent, we have as yet no explanation for its existence. But then we cannot have a *sufficient* explanation for A and B, since they depend on C. Demea's point is precisely that however we extend the chain, we never get a *sufficient* explanation for any of its links.

Cleanthes' other criticism is also fallacious. It depends on an absolute dichotomy between the analytic or a priori on the one hand and the synthetic or a posteriori on the other. A statement which is analytic or a priori may be necessary but it applies only to our ideas, not to the world. A statement which is synthetic or a posteriori may apply to the world but it cannot be necessary. The idea of necessary existence which is involved in Demea's argument is therefore confused. Necessity cannot apply to existence but only to our ideas. Now this dichotomy is not a neutral classification; it is a mere reflection of the empiricist philosophy. Thus it is simply presupposed that any belief about the world must be contingent, so that one can know its truth only by checking against the world whether it happens to be so. In the first place, that is the point at issue. But, in the second, the view presupposed is in any case incoherent. Unless one already has some knowledge of the world, one cannot check any belief against it. It is impossible that *every* belief should be checked in that way.

Hume's commitment to the above dichotomy is perhaps the greatest among his many inconsistencies. For, as Kant pointed out, he had already undermined the dichotomy in his analysis of causality. Thus a belief in causality is not analytic. But neither is it simply a posteriori. For prior to our experience of an event, we *already* believe it will have a cause. We may add that the dichotomy is inadequate to explain any of our fundamental beliefs. Take our belief in an independent world. This belief is not logically necessary, for it may be denied without formal contradiction. But whenever we check a belief empirically, we *already* presuppose the existence of an independent world. Hume is committed to a dichotomy which, *on his own showing*, is inadequate to explain any of our fundamental beliefs. Here there is a radical conflict between his empiricism and his naturalism.

In Parts X and XI, the discussion moves on to ground where Philo is entirely at home. Supposing that from the order of the world we can infer the existence of God, can we infer also his perfect wisdom and goodness?

Look around this universe. What an immense profusion of beings, animated and organised, sensible and active! You admire this prodigious variety and fecundity. But inspect a little more narrowly these living existences, the only beings worth regarding. How hostile and

126

destructive to each other! How insufficient all of them for their own happiness! How contemptible or odious to the spectator! The whole presents nothing but the idea of a blind nature, impregnated by a great vivifying principle, and pouring forth from her lap, without discernment or parental care, her maimed and abortive children.[32]

Is the purpose in this easily recognizable as wise and good? Indeed, is there in this anything easily recognizable as even analogous to human purpose?

> Here, Cleanthes, I find myself at ease in my argument. Here I triumph. Formerly, when we argued concerning the natural attributes of intelligence and design, I needed all my sceptical and metaphysical subtilty to elude your grasp. In many views of the universe, and of its parts, particularly the latter, the beauty and fitness of final causes strike us with such irresistible force, that all objections appear (what I believe they really are) mere cavils and sophisms, nor can we then imagine how it was ever possible for us to repose any weight on them. But there is no view of human life, or of the condition of mankind, from which, without the greatest violence, we can infer the moral attributes, or learn that infinite benevolence, conjoined with infinite power and infinite wisdom, which we must discover by the eyes of faith alone. It is your turn now to tug the labouring oar, and to support your philosophical subtilties against the dictates of plain reason and experience.[33]

The above passage is significant for the light it throws on the purpose of the *Dialogues* as a whole. Here Philo makes explicit what has already been implied, that he does not wish to deny the force of the argument from design. What he denies is that in this way one can infer a God whose nature conforms to the popular model. The order of the world does not conform to human purpose nor can it be measured by any human conception of good and evil. At every point it is transcendent.

Part XII concludes the work by making the above point fully explicit. Philo proceeds to a powerful affirmation of the argument from design.

> *That nature does nothing in vain*, is a maxim established in all the schools, merely from that contemplation of the works of nature, without any religious purpose; and, from a firm conviction of its truth, an anatomist, who had observed a new organ or canal, would never be satisfied till he had also discovered its use and intention. One great foundation of the Copernican system is the maxim, *that nature acts by the simplest methods, and chooses the most proper means to any end*; and astronomers often, without thinking of it, lay this strong foundation of piety and religion. The same thing is observable in

other parts of Philosophy. And thus all the sciences lead us insensibly to acknowledge a first intelligent Author; and their authority is often so much the greater, as they do not directly profess that intention.[34]

After elaborating this point, Philo proceeds to argue that the dispute between theist and atheist is merely verbal. Each merely emphasizes different aspects of the same truth. Many commentators interpret this as a subtle ploy by which Philo renounces what he has only just affirmed. Thus his affirmation – or so they argue – is so immediately qualified that it becomes indistinguishable from atheism. Indeed, the difference between the two is merely verbal. But that is entirely to misunderstand Philo's argument. In fact the reconciliation between theism and atheism is achieved not by renouncing theism but by transforming atheism into eighteenth-century deism. Let us consider the relevant passage.

> I next turn to the atheist, who, I assent, is only nominally so, and can never possibly be in earnest; and I ask him, whether, from the coherence and apparent sympathy in all the parts of this world, there be not a certain degree of analogy among all the operations of nature, in every situation and in every age; whether the rotting of a turnip, the generation of an animal and the structure of human thought be not energies that probably bear some remote analogy to each other: It is impossible he can deny it: he will readily acknowledge it. *Having obtained this concession, I push him still further in his retreat; and I ask him, if it be not probable that the principle which first arranged and still maintains, order in this universe, bears not also some remote inconceivable analogy to the other operations of nature, and among the rest to the economy of the human mind and thought. However reluctant, he must give his assent.*[my emphasis][35]

Now any full-blooded atheist would surely remain on the level of the rotting turnip, the generation of animals and the structure of human thought. In other words, he would treat the natural world as ultimate. Hume's atheist, by contrast, is prepared to acknowledge a principle which transcends that world, which first arranged and still maintains it and which therefore serves as the source and explanation for its order. In short, he is indistinguishable from an eighteenth-century deist.

A little reflection will reveal that Philo's treatment of atheism is entirely compatible with what he has just affirmed. The point to grasp is that what we now take seriously as atheism would scarcely in the eighteenth century have been taken seriously at all. For us an atheist is one who holds that the whole universe is the product of nothing but chance and blind causation. But that view did not get its grip on the educated imagination until late in the nineteenth century, when people became acquainted with the theory of evolution.[36] To Hume, the view was as implausible as it was to the rest of his contemporaries. For him, atheism was plausible only when it took the form of rejecting the anthropomorphic God of vulgar superstition. But remove God in that form and, so far as Hume is concerned, there is nothing left to debate. For who can seriously deny that there is an ultimate source of order and who can deny that this is what in natural theology is called God?

Philo has now completed the strictly philosophical part of his argument.

> These, Cleanthes, are my unfeigned sentiments on this subject; and these sentiments, you know, I have ever cherished and maintained. But in proportion to my veneration for true religion, is my abhorrence of vulgar superstitions; and I indulge a peculiar pleasure, I confess, in pushing such principles, sometimes into absurdity, sometimes into impiety. And you are sensible, that all bigots, notwithstanding their great aversion to the latter above the former, are commonly equally guilty of both.[37]

Philo now launches himself into a full scale denunciation of popular religion, or, as he terms it, vulgar superstition. He is not entirely consistent. For example, at one point, he argues that morality does not require the support of religion. The hope of everlasting happiness is little inducement to virtue. It is too remote. People hardly ever think of an after-life, being almost exclusively concerned with their immediate circumstances. But at another point, he castigates the churches for preaching the fires of hell, thereby causing terror and despair. It is difficult to see how the fires of hell can cause terror and despair among people who almost never think about an after-life. On the other hand, if they do think seriously about an after-life, it is difficult to believe that they find no inducement in the hope of everlasting happiness. When it is a question of doing good, popular religion may be excluded for it has little effect in men's minds. But it is pregnant with such effects when the question arises of whether it may do harm. Hume makes the elementary error of supposing that the more he blackens his opponents, the more the reader will sympathize with his views. In fact, the writer who adopts this procedure usually elicits in his reader a sympathy not for himself but for his opponent. Philo ends his denunciation on a note familiar amongst eighteenth-century deists.

> *To know God*, says Seneca, *is to worship him*. All other worship is indeed absurd, superstitious, and even impious. It degrades him to the low condition of mankind, who are delighted with entreaty, solicitation, presents, and flattery. Yet is this impiety the smallest of which superstition is guilty. Commonly, it depresses the Deity far below the condition of mankind; and represents him as a capricious Daemon, who exercises his power without reason and without humanity! And were that divine Being disposed to be offended by the vices and

follies of silly mortals, who are his own workmanship; ill would it surely fare with the votaries of most popular superstitions. Nor would any of human race merit his *favour*, but a very few, the philosophical theists, who entertain, or rather indeed endeavour to entertain, suitable notions of his divine perfections: As the only persons entitled to his *compassion* and *indulgence* would be the philosophical sceptics, a sect almost equally rare, who, from a natural diffidence of their own capacity, suspend, or endeavour to suspend all judgement with regard to such sublime and such extraordinary subjects.[38]

Anxious not to lend support in any way to the forces of superstition, Hume completes his work by expressing his conclusion in the most negative terms possible. He will go no further than a God who is the source of order in the universe and who bears, perhaps, some remote analogy to human intelligence. On the other hand, if the proposition is thus confined:

If it affords no inference that affects human life, or can be the source of any action or forbearance: And if the analogy, imperfect as it is, can be carried no further than to the human intelligence; and cannot be transferred with any appearance of probability, to the other qualities of the mind: If this really be the case, what can the most inquisitive, contemplative, and religious man do more than give a plain philosophical assent to the proposition, as often as it occurs; and believe that the arguments, on which it is established, exceed the objections which lie against it?[39]

9

CONCLUSION

On the empiricist view, we reason on the basis of beliefs which are justified by sense experience. On the naturalist, we can justify beliefs by sense experience only because we already have beliefs and, consequently, there is more in our beliefs than sense experience can explain or justify. The empiricist, at his most extreme, holds that the natural world falls entirely within the categories of chance and blind causation and that the source of knowledge is therefore entirely in ourselves. The naturalist, by contrast, holds that our knowledge presupposes an intelligible order, not of our own making, which is common to nature and ourselves.

In the eighteenth century, empiricism was the dominant philosophy in Britain. At the beginning of the nineteenth century, it was some form of naturalism which flourished. Hume's philosophy was of decisive importance in producing the change. For it seemed evident, however he was interpreted, that he had revealed the bankruptcy of eighteenth-century empiricism. Whether or not he was a sceptic, he had shown that our fundamental beliefs cannot be explained in empiricist terms. Consequently, our ability to know the world through sense experience was no longer seen as the solution to the problem of knowledge. It was itself a problem. The question was: *how* is it possible to know the world through sense experience? Kant and the Scottish naturalists arrived independently at similar solutions. Sense experience is unintelligible except within categories or forms of belief which in the empiricist sense are a priori. Unless we are already adjusted to know the world, we cannot know it through sense experience. At the beginning of the nineteenth century, this view was dominant both in Britain and on the continent.

A change occurred in the middle of the nineteenth century. In Britain this was due to the influence of J. S. Mill.[1] Mill had inherited from his father a version of eighteenth-century empiricism. He took the philosophy of Kant and of the Scottish naturalists to be a form of obscurantist intuitionism which in political and social affairs assisted the party of reaction. The interpretation was entirely dubious. For example, Kant and William Hamilton, the leader of the Scottish school, were both liberals and no one has shown that their liberalism was incompatible with their philosophy. Nevertheless, Mill thought their philosophy reactionary and, both in his book on logic and in his study of William Hamilton's philosophy, he took it upon himself, in the name of empiricism, to launch an attack on the whole school. The works exerted an enormous influence and Mill's attack was generally thought to be successful. As a result, empiricism, once again, became the dominant philosophy in Britain. It has remained so until the present day. There has been only one exceptional period. Towards the end of the nineteenth century, T. H. Green argued, with considerable power, that it was Mill who was the real reactionary. For, in effect, he had taken philosophy back to the eighteenth century, reinstating views which had been undermined by Hume and comprehensively refuted by his successors. But Green's influence was brief. In the present century, Russell adopted a philosophy comparable with Mill's, and his successors, A. J. Ayer and the logical positivists, adopted a form of empiricism even more extreme than that of the eighteenth century. Moreover, although empiricism in a form that extreme has been abandoned, it has been replaced by varieties of scientific naturalism which have very much more in common with empiricism than with the naturalism of the Scottish school.[2]

A study of the conflict in Hume's philosophy between empiricism and naturalism is therefore of interest not simply in its own right but also because of the light it throws on the history of philosophy. It prefigures the conflict between the two views which occurred during the succeeding century. What I have argued, in effect, is that Kant, Hamilton and Green were correct and that the triumph of empiricism has proved a misfortune for philosophy. For Hume's philosophy does indeed show the bankruptcy of empiricism. Wherever he reasons consistently with his empiricist assumptions, he finds himself involved in insoluble problems. Wherever he rises above those problems, he reasons consistently with the principles of Scottish naturalism. This is as true of the *Dialogues* as of the *Treatise*. The sceptical sections of the *Dialogues* are all based on a view of science derived from eighteenth-century empiricism. Yet here again, he raises above outright scepticism and is prepared, in however muted or limited a fashion, to affirm what those assumptions would lead him to deny.

If I am correct, we must take a fresh look at the history of philosophy during the last two or three centuries. That history, in any case, has been written almost exclusively from the point of view of those who accept the empiricism of Mill and his successors. There is a different story to be told and within it we may expect the Scottish school to receive an acknowledgement more adequate to its merits.

NOTES

1 INTRODUCTION: THE SCHOLARLY BACKGROUND

1 *The Philosophy of David Hume*, London, Macmillan, 1941.
2 The main works by Thomas Reid (1710–1796) are *An Inquiry into the Human Mind on the Principles of Common Sense, Essays on the Intellectual Powers of Man* and *Essays on the Active Powers of Man*. The main works of T. H. Green (1836–1882) are *Lectures on the Principles of Political Obligation, Prolegomena to Ethics* and *Introductions to Hume's Treatise of Human Nature* (reprinted as *Hume and Locke*).
3 *The Works of Thomas Reid, D D*, Vols I and II, Sir William Hamilton (ed.), London, Longman, 1863, Vol. II, p. 760.
4 For this reason he was the favourite philosopher of J. G. Hamann, the great enemy of the enlightenment. See the study by Isaiah Berlin: *The Magus of the North*, Glasgow, Fontana Press, 1994.
5 *A Treatise of Human Nature*, L. A. Selby-Biggs and P. H. Nidditch (eds), Oxford, The Clarendon Press, 1978, Book I, Part IV, p. 187.
6 Kemp Smith mentions the resemblances between Hume and Kant but he does not make as much of these resemblances as he might have done. The reason for this will presently emerge. The works by Immanuel Kant (1724–1804) which are relevant to this study are the *Critique of Pure Reason, Groundwork of the Metaphysics of Morals* and *Prolegomena to any Future Metaphysic*.
7 *An Inquiry Concerning Human Understanding*, Charles W. Hendel (ed.), New York, The Liberal Arts Press, 1957, p. 170.
8 He had published a sketch of his view much earlier in *Mind* Vols 54 and 55, 1905. But it was not until 1941 that he attempted to substantiate his view in detail.
9 *Treatise*, Book I, Part IV, p. 217.
10 For an alternative view in the recent literature see Don Garrett's *Cognition and Commitment in Hume's Philosophy*, New York, OUP, 1997. Garrett's project is to show that Hume had a single coherent philosophy of the empiricist type. My objections to this project will emerge as this study proceeds. Nevertheless I have profited from reading Garrett's stimulating work.
11 *Treatise*, Book I, Part I, p. 86.
12 *Treatise*, Book I, Part III, p. 165.
13 *The Dictionary of Philosophy and Psychology*, J. M. Baldwin (ed.), 3 vols, Gloucester, Mass., 1960, Vol. 2, pp. 137–138.
14 *The Philosophy of David Hume*, Norman Kemp Smith, London, Macmillan, 1941, p. 52.
15 See Barry Stroud's *Hume*, London, Routledge and Kegan Paul, 1977, pp. 8–9.

16 *David Hume*, Princeton, NJ, Princeton University Press, 1982.
17 The full quotation runs as follows: 'Hume and Reid differed in substance as well as words, for Hume rejected that supernaturally founded or motivated reliance on natural belief – that curious supernatural naturalism – which characterizes the work of Reid and the other Scots' (ibid., p. 208).
18 Ibid., pp. 202–203.
19 Ibid., pp. 203–204.
20 Ibid., p. 180.
21 *Essays on the Intellectual Powers of Man*, A. D. Woozley (ed.), Macmillan, 1941, pp. 181–182.
22 It is by no means the only place where he does so. He affirms the validity of the argument from design in *The Natural History of Religion*, which was written around the same time as the *Dialogues*. Indeed the central argument of that work presupposes that God's existence can be established on rational grounds. A few years previously, in *A Letter from a Gentleman*, which is perhaps the clearest exposition of his views, he affirmed quite emphatically that the argument from design is valid. See *A Letter from a Gentleman to his Friend in Edinburgh*, E. C. Mossner and J. V. Price (eds), Edinburgh, The University of Edinburgh, 1967, p. 25. I am grateful to Ian Tipton for drawing my attention to this work.

2 AIMS AND METHODS IN THE *TREATISE*

1 We may note that Locke, also, adopted a similar method.
2 *The Mathematical Principles of Natural Philosophy*, trans. F. Cajori, Berkeley, University of California Press, 1946, pp. 543 sq.
3 The main works by René Descartes (1596–1650) are the *Meditations*, *Discourse on Method* and *Principles of Philosophy*.
4 *Treatise*, p. xix.
5 P. Duhem, *The Aim and Structure of Physical Theory*, trans. P. Wiener, New York, Atheneum, 1962, pp. 191–196.
6 *Treatise*, p. xiv.
7 Ibid., p. xv.
8 Ibid., p. xvii.
9 Ibid., p. xviii.

3 EMPIRICIST ASSUMPTIONS

1 It is worth noting that Kant was aware of Reid's views but seems not to have read him. Scottish naturalism is sometimes referred to as the philosophy of common sense. Kant took this to mean that for Reid and the others, one should solve philosophical problems by consulting the opinions of ordinary people. In fact, they were referring to ideas or beliefs common alike to the learned and the vulgar. Roughly speaking, they were referring to those categories which for Kant are fundamental to all thought. Kant's view of the history of philosophy was often eccentric. For example, he took Berkeley to be an *explicit* sceptic. According to Kant, his deliberate aim was to undermine our belief in the independent world. In fact, it is obvious that Berkeley took himself, rightly or wrongly, to be *defending* that view. Manfred Kuehn, however, suggests that after Kant had written his main work, *The Critique of Pure Reason*, he may have come to a better understanding of Reid's views and that certain revisions in later editions of that work may even have been influenced by him. See 'Reid's Contribution to "Hume's Problem"' in *The Science of Man in the Scottish Enlightenment*, P. Jones (ed.), Edinburgh,

Edinburgh University Press, 1989. This collection also contains an excellent discussion by Keith Lehrer of the differences between Reid and Hume. See 'Beyond Impressions and Ideas: Hume v. Reid'.

2 *Treatise*, pp. 12–13.

3 Throughout this chapter I have assumed that Hume's empiricism is of the subjective or traditional type. The reader may wish to note that some recent commentators do not share that view. For example, D. W. Livingstone denies that Hume held a subjective view of experience (see *Hume's Philosophy of Common Life*, Chicago, University of Chicago Press, 1984, p. 63). On Livingstone's view, Hume uses 'experience' in a popular sense where it is roughly equivalent to the general use of our faculties in engagement with the world. He fails to note, however, that when 'experience' is used that widely, it becomes for philosophical purposes entirely useless. Thus in our general engagement with the world we exhibit powers or abilities that are difficult to explain on any doctrine hitherto called empiricist. For example, we can arrive at conclusions about the world as it existed prior to all human experience. The empiricist owes us an explanation for these powers or abilities. He cannot discharge this debt simply by shifting the label 'experience' to include them in his doctrine.

By contrast, empiricism in the traditional form gives 'experience' a definite content, confining its reference to the sensory states involved in the exercise of the sense organs. Experience in this sense is treated as the source of all knowledge. Other faculties of the mind are treated as subordinate. For example, memory is treated as a device by which experiences in the past are preserved in the present, inference as the mode by which we move from present experiences to those in the future, and so on. This doctrine has definite content. Unfortunately it is catastrophic in its consequences. It is precisely the effect of this doctrine on Hume's naturalism that I explore in this study.

For an extensive criticism of the empiricist theory of meaning see P. Geach, *Mental Acts*, London, Routledge and Kegan Paul, 1971.

4 CAUSATION

1 *Treatise*, p. 74.
2 Ibid., p. 77.
3 Ibid., p. 93.
4 Ibid., p. 91.
5 Ibid., p. 94.
6 Ibid., p. 156.
7 Ibid., p. 88.
8 Ibid., p. 156.
9 Ibid., p. 168.
10 This is a point rightly emphasized by G. Strawson in his book *The Secret Connexion*, Oxford, The Clarendon Press, 1989. He uses the point, however, to argue that Hume is not committed to a strictly empiricist theory of meaning. As David Pears has shown, this interpretation is in conflict with the analysis of perception which Hume gives, for example, in discussing our idea of an independent world. See D. Pears, *Hume's System*, Oxford, OUP, 1990, pp. 91–92.

Don Garrett, by contrast, argues that there is no incompatibility between holding an empiricist theory of meaning and employing the idea that there are features of the world which transcend human experience (op. cit. p. 114). But this seems evidently false. It is plainly impossible for a human being to derive an idea of features transcending human experience, when that idea has to be a *copy* of what he has experienced, or be resolvable into simple ideas, each of which is similarly a mere *copy*. There is no doubt that Hume employs such an idea. Indeed, it is central to his philosophy. But that shows his inconsistency.

11 *Treatise*, pp. 165–166.
12 Ibid., p. 170.
13 Ibid., p. 94.
14 *Prolegomena to any Future Metaphysic*, trans. J. W. Ellington, Indianapolis, Hackett Publishing Company, 1976, p. 5.
15 Op. cit., p. 638.
16 This is the view of causality most commonly defended by modern empiricists. It has been defended in detail, for example, by A. J. Ayer and J. L. Mackie.
17 As we have seen, Hume associated this view especially with the Cartesians.
18 This would be the view, for example, of the Greek Sceptics.

5 SCEPTICISM

1 There are a number of studies which discuss the role of scepticism in Hume's philosophy. See, for example, R. J. Fogelin, *Hume's Skepticism in the Treatise of Human Nature*, London, Routledge and Kegan Paul, 1985.
2 Ibid., p. 183.
3 This is a point that D. W. Livingstone is rightly concerned to emphasize throughout the work cited earlier.
4 Ibid., p. 187.
5 Ibid., p. 189.
6 Ibid., p. 193.
7 When Hume refers, in this section, to the views of the philosophers, he primarily has in mind the views of Descartes and Locke.
8 Ibid., p. 222.
9 Ibid., p. 213–214.
10 Ibid., p. 264.
11 Ibid., p. 269.
12 Ibid., p. 270.
13 Ibid., p. 271.
14 Ibid., p. 270.

6 THE PASSIONS

1 For alternative studies which discuss Hume's view of the passions, see P. S. Árdall, *Passion and Value in Hume's Treatise*, Edinburgh, Edinburgh University Press, 1966, and A. C. Baier, *A Progress of Sentiments: Reflections on Hume's Treatise*, Cambridge, Mass., Harvard University Press, 1991.
2 We refer to a pure sensation, one which calls attention to itself. As it enters into certain of our faculties, sensation can take a more active role. We have noted the point in connection with perception.
3 Ibid., p. 401.
4 Ibid., p. 403.
5 Ibid., p. 406.
6 Ibid., p. 410.
7 Ibid., p. 409–410.
8 Ibid., p. 413.
9 Ibid., p. 415.
10 Ibid., p. 416.

11 Ibid., p. 416.
12 *An Inquiry Concerning Human Understanding*, pp. 67–68.

7 REASON AND MORALITY

1 For alternative views of Hume's moral philosophy, see J. L. Mackie, *Hume's Moral Theory*, London, Routledge and Kegan Paul, 1980, and J. Harrison, *Hume's Moral Epistemology*, Oxford, The Clarendon Press, 1976.
2 *Treatise*, pp. 456–457.
3 The main work by Francis Hutcheson (1694–1747) is *Inquiry into the Original of Our Ideas of Beauty and Virtue*.
4 *Illustrations Upon The Moral Sense* in *Philosophical Writings*, Everyman, 1994, p. 131.
5 For our purpose, the main work by Jeremy Bentham (1748–1832) is *An Introduction to the Principles of Morals and Legislation*.
6 *Treatise*, p. 467.
7 Ibid., pp. 468–469.
8 Ibid., pp. 469–470.
9 See, for example, A. J. Ayer, *Language Truth and Logic*, Gollancz, 1946, and C. L. Stevenson, *Ethics and Language*, Yale University Press, 1944. See also, J.-P. Sartre, *Existentialism and Humanism*, Methuen, 1948, p. 31: 'If a voice speaks to me, it is still I myself who must decide whether the voice is or is not that of an angel. If I regard a certain course of action as good, it is only I who choose to say that it is good and not bad.'
10 For a further discussion of this issue, see V. C. Chappell, *et al.* (eds), *Hume*, New York, Doubleday, 1966.
11 See *The Language of Morals*, Oxford, The Clarendon Press, 1952.
12 *Treatise*, p. 471.
13 Ibid., p. 472.
14 Ibid., p. 473.
15 The main work by Thomas Hobbes (1588–1679) is *Leviathan*, one of the acknowledged classics in political philosophy.
16 Ibid., p. 478.
17 Ibid., p. 479.
18 Ibid., p. 479.
19 Ibid., p. 481.
20 Ibid., p. 486.
21 Ibid., p. 486.
22 Ibid., p. 489.
23 Ibid., p. 490.

8 REASON AND THEOLOGY

1 For example, in a recent edition of the work, it is said to constitute, along with the *Natural History of Religion* 'the most formidable attack on the rationality of religious belief ever mounted by a philosopher'. See *Dialogues and the Natural History of Religion*, J. C. A. Gaskin (ed.), The World's Classics, OUP, 1993.
2 See John Calvin (1509–1564) *Institutes of the Christian Religion*, trans. H. Beveridge, Grand Rapids, Eerdmans, 1989.
3 The main work of Thomas Aquinas (*c.* 1225–1274) is the *Summa Theologiae*.
4 Brian Davies, *The Thought of Thomas Aquinas*, Oxford, The Clarendon Press, 1992, p. 21.
5 Ibid., p. 41.

6   *Thomas Aquinas: Philosophical Texts*, ed. Thomas Gilby, Oxford, 1951, p. 88.
7   Ibid., p. 63.
8   J. H. Newman, *An Essay on the Development of Christian Doctrine*, J. M. Cameron (ed.), Penguin, 1974, p. 343.
9   For our purpose, the main works by John Locke (1632–1704) are *An Essay Concerning Human Understanding* and *The Reasonableness of Christianity*.
10 *Dialogues and the Natural History of Religion*, The World's Classics, OUP, p. 40.
11 Newman, op. cit., p. 344. Readers of William James will note that Newman's criticism of Locke may well have provided the inspiration for his celebrated paper, *The Will to Believe*.
12 William Paley (1743–1805) is best known for his *Evidences of Christianity* and *Natural Theology, or Evidences of the Existence and Attributes of the Deity Collected from the Appearances of Nature*.
13 For a brilliant and vitriolic account of this movement see H. L. Mansel's article 'Freethinking – Its History And Tendencies' in *Letters, Lectures and Reviews*, London, John Murray, 1873, reprinted by Thoemmes, 1990.
14 It is worth emphasizing that I should not simply identify William Paley's argument with the argument in its popular form, though the two are easily associated. Paley's argument is more sophisticated than it is often made to appear.
15 *In Soft Garments*, London, The Catholic Book Club, 1941, p. 2.
16 *Dialogues Concerning Natural Religion*, The World's Classics edn, OUP, pp. 116–117.
17 Ibid., p. 130.
18 D. F. Norton implies in the work already cited that Hume's commitment to natural belief does not extend to religious or metaphysical issues. For a criticism of this view see T. Penelhum's *God and Skepticism*, Dordrecht, Kluwer, 1983, pp. 139–144. To be recommended also is the section on religion in his *Hume*, London, Macmillan, 1975. His view that Hume has utterly discredited natural theology seems to be a product of that empiricism which I have attempted to expose in this study. Nevertheless, his discussion of the issues is lively and informative.
19 *Dialogues*, p. 56.
20 Ibid., p. 57.
21 *Enquiries*, p. 148.
22 Ibid., p. 46.
23 Ibid., p. 118.
24 Ibid., p. 116.
25 *Dialogues and the Natural History of Religion*, The World's Classics, OUP, pp. 33–34.
26 Ibid., p. 45.
27 Ibid., p. 55.
28 *Dialogues Concerning Natural Religion*, K. Smith (ed.) New York, Bobbs-Merrill, 1947, p. 101.
29 The inadequacy of Kemp Smith's criticism at this point has been exposed by a number of commentators. See, for example, Stanley Tweyman's introduction to the *Dialogues Concerning Natural Religion*, London, Routledge, 1991.
30 *Dialogues*, pp. 56–57.
31 Ibid., p. 61.
32 Ibid., p. 113.
33 Ibid., p. 104.
34 Ibid., pp. 116–117.
35 Ibid., p. 120.
36 The view itself may be traced back to the Greek atomists. But before the nineteenth century it was held only by a minority, even among educated people.

37 Ibid., p. 121.
38 Ibid., pp. 128–129.
39 Ibid., p. 129.

9 CONCLUSION

1 For our purpose, the main work by J. S. Mill (1806–1873) is *An Examination of Sir William Hamilton's Philosophy*.
2 An exception is the work of Wittgenstein which has obvious resemblances to that of Reid and Hamilton. For example, the following remarks of Hamilton's might have served as a motto for Wittgenstein's *On Certainty*: 'belief is the primary condition of reason and not reason the ultimate ground of belief'.

BIBLIOGRAPHY

Alexander, P., *Sensationalism and Scientific Explanation*, London, Routledge and Kegan Paul, 1963.

Aquinas, T., *Thomas Aquinas: Philosophical Texts*, J. Gilby (ed.), London, Oxford University Press, 1951.

Árdall, P. S., *Passion and Value in Hume's Treatise*, Edinburgh, Edinburgh University Press, 1966.

Ayer, A. J., *Hume*, Oxford, OUP, 1980.

—— *Language, Truth and Logic*, London, Gollancz, 1946.

Baier, A. C., *A Progress of Sentiments: Reflections on Hume's Treatise*, Cambridge, Mass., Harvard University Press, 1991.

Beauchamp, T. and Rosenburg, A., *Hume and the Problem of Causation*, Oxford, OUP, 1981.

Bentham, J., *An Introduction to the Principles of Morals and Legislation*, Oxford, The Clarendon Press, 1823.

Berlin, I., *The Magus of the North*, Glasgow, Fontana Press, 1994.

Calvin, J., *Institutes of Christian Religion*, trans. H. Beveridge, Grand Rapids, Eerdmans, 1989.

Chappell, V. C., *et al.*, *Hume*, V. C. Chappell (ed.), New York, Doubleday, 1966.

Davies, B., *The Thought of Thomas Aquinas*, Oxford, The Clarendon Press, 1992.

Descartes, R., *Selected Philosophical Writings*, trans. J. Cottingham, R. Stoothoff and D. Murdoch, Cambridge, CUP, 1988.

Duhem, P., *The Aim and Structure of Physical Theory*, trans. P. Wiener, New York, Atheneum, 1962.

Flew, A., *Hume's Philosophy of Belief*, London, Routledge and Kegan Paul, 1961.

Fogelin, R. J., *Hume's Skepticism in the Treatise of Human Nature*, London, Routledge and Kegan Paul, 1985.

Garrett, D., *Cognition and Commitment in Hume's Philosophy*, New York, OUP, 1997.

Geach, P., *Mental Acts*, London, Routledge and Kegan Paul, 1971.

Green, T. H., *Hume and Locke*, New York, Thomas Cromwell, 1968.

Hare, R. M., *The Language of Morals*, Oxford, The Clarendon Press, 1952.

Harrison, J., *Hume's Moral Epistemology*, Oxford, The Clarendon Press, 1976.

Hobbes, T, *Leviathan*, M. Oakeshott (ed.), Oxford, Blackwell, 1947.

Hume, D., *An Abstract of a Treatise of Human Nature*, J. M. Keynes and P. Sraffa (eds), Cambridge, CUP, 1938.

—— *Dialogues Concerning Natural Religion*, Kemp Smith (ed.), New York, Bobbs-Merrill, 1947.

—— *Dialogues Concerning Natural Religion*, Stanley Tweyman (ed.), London, Routledge, 1991.

—— *Dialogues and the Natural History of Religion*, J. C. A. Gaskin (ed.), Oxford, The World's Classics, OUP, 1993.

—— *An Inquiry Concerning Human Understanding*, C. W. Hendel (ed.), New York, Liberal Arts Press, 1957.

—— *A Letter from a Gentleman to his Friend in Edinburgh*, E. C. Mossner and J. V. Price (eds), Edinburgh, The University of Edinburgh, 1967.

—— *A Treatise of Human Nature*, L. A. Selby-Biggs and P. H. Nidditch (eds), Oxford, The Clarendon Press, 1978.

Jenkins, J., *Understanding Hume*, Edinburgh, Edinburgh University Press, 1992.

Jones, P., *Hume's Sentiments, Their Ciceronian and French Context*, Edinburgh, Edinburgh University Press, 1982.

—— (ed.) *The Science of Man in the Scottish Enlightenment*, Edinburgh, Edinburgh University Press, 1989.

Kant, I., *Critique of Pure Reason*, trans. Kemp Smith, London, Macmillan, 1929.

—— *The Moral Law: Groundwork of the Metaphysics of Morals*, trans. H. J. Paton, London, Routledge, 1989.

—— *Prolegomena to any Future Metaphysic*, trans. J. W. Ellington, Indianapolis, Hackett Publishing Company, 1976.

Knox, R., *In Soft Garments*, London, The Catholic Book Club, 1941.

Lehrer, K., *Thomas Reid*, London, Routledge, 1989.

Livingston, D. W., *Hume's Philosophy of Common Life*, Chicago, University of Chicago Press, 1984.

Locke, J., *An Essay Concerning Human Understanding*, P. H. Nidditch (ed.), Oxford, The Clarendon Press, 1975.

—— *The Reasonableness of Christianity*, Collected Works, Vol. 7, Glasgow, R. Griffin and Co., 1823.

Mackie, J. L., 'Causes and Conditions', *American Philosophical Quarterly*, No. 2, 1965.

—— *Hume's Moral Theory*, London, Routledge and Kegan Paul, 1980.

Mansell, H. L., *Letters, Lectures and Reviews*, Bristol, Thoemmes, 1990.

Mill, J. S., *An Examination of Sir William Hamilton's Philosophy*, J. M. Robson (ed.), Collected Works, Vol. IX, Toronto, University of Toronto Press, 1979.

Mossner, E. C., *The Life of David Hume*, 2nd edn, Oxford, The Clarendon Press, 1980.

Newman, J. H., *An Essay on the Development of Christian Doctrine*, J. M. Cameron (ed.), London, Penguin, 1974.

Newton, I., *The Mathematical Principles of Natural Philosophy*, trans. F. Cajori, Berkeley, University of California Press, 1946.

Norton, D. F., *David Hume: Common Sense Moralist Sceptical Metaphysician*, Princeton, NJ, Princeton University Press, 1982.

Paley, W., *Natural Theology: Selections*, F. Ferré (ed.), Indianapolis, Bobbs-Merrill, 1963.

Passmore, J., *Hume's Intentions*, Cambridge, CUP, 1952.

Pears, D., *Hume's System*, Oxford, OUP, 1990.

Penelhum, T., *God and Skepticism*, Dordrecht, Kluwer, 1983.

—— *Hume*, London, Macmillan, 1975.

Price, H. H., *Hume's Theory of the External World*, Oxford, OUP, 1963.

Reid, T., *Essays on the Intellectual Powers of Man*, A. D. Woozley (ed.), London, Macmillan, 1941.

—— *Essays on the Active Powers of Man*, Cambridge, Mass., MIT, 1969.

—— *An Inquiry into the Human Mind on the Principles of Common Sense*, Chicago, University of Chicago Press, 1970.

—— *The Works of Thomas Reid D D*, Vols I and II, Sir William Hamilton (ed.), London, Longman, 1863.

Sartre, J.-P., *Existentialism and Humanism*, London, Methuen, 1948.

Smith, N. K., 'The Naturalism of Hume', *Mind*, Vol. XIV, 1905.

—— *The Philosophy of David Hume*, London, Macmillan, 1941.

Stevenson, C. L., *Ethics and Language*, Yale, Conn., Yale University Press, 1944.

Stove, D. C., *Probability and Hume's Inductive Scepticism*, Oxford, The Clarendon Press, 1973.

Strawson, G., *The Secret Connexion*, Oxford, The Clarendon Press, 1989.

Stroud, B., *Hume*, London, Routledge and Kegan Paul, 1977.

Swinburne, R., *The Existence of God*, Oxford, The Clarendon Press, 1979.

INDEX